Derbyshire Portraits

by
Clarence Daniel

Dalesman Books
1978

The Dalesman Publishing Company Ltd.,
Clapham (via Lancaster), North Yorkshire

First published 1978

ISBN: 0 85206 470 5

Printed in Great Britain by
va Printing Co. Ltd., Hallam Road, Nelson, Lancashire

CONTENTS

The portrait sketches are by Margaret Sandell and Jill M. Beswick. The cover sketches show Caroline Ann Smedley (front) and Samuel Fox (back).

Preface

THE original purpose of this book was to provide a series of biographical sketches of some of Derbyshire's 'little women' who figure in a talk which has provoked the curiosity and interest of feminine organisations.

Much has been written about such personalities as Bess of Hardwick who wrote her proud signature in stone here and there in the county, or the charming Georgiana, Duchess of Devonshire, of whom a famous artist exclaimed in exasperation when painting her portrait, 'Your Grace is too hard for me!' Many people will be familiar with the name of Florence Nightingale, heroine of the Scutari military hospitals during the Crimean War, or perhaps with that of Catherine Mompesson whose devotion to her husband resulted in her death from bubonic plague. The name of Anna Seward, 'Swan of Lichfield', will be known to more serious students of county literature, and the name of Catherine Mumford, of Ashbourne, is still remembered as wife of William Booth, founder of the Salvation Army.

But the 'little women' I had singled out were some of the minor characters whose names have inadvertantly found their way (in small print, as it were) into the pages of Derbyshire history books. Some of them, I am sure, never dreamed that they would be remembered beyond their own day and generation, but for one reason or another they were.

It was then felt that some male personalities should be included in the selection, and perhaps some of these are of a less minor category in that several have become household words. But this may give a better balance to the book and widen its appeal to the general reader.

I would like to express my gratitude to Mrs. Margaret Sandell and Miss Jill Beswick for the excellent portrait studies they have provided as illustration and which have greatly enriched the text of this book.

Joan Waste
The Derby Martyr

OVER four hundred years ago a 'poore honest godlie woman' was burnt at the stake in Derby for refusing to renounce her Protestant convictions. She was only twenty-two years old and her story is all the more tragic because she had never seen the faces of her father, mother, brother or friends. She had often heard the crash of thunder, but had never seen the vivid streak of forked lightning; often she had felt the warmth of the sun, but had never watched its burning orb dissolve into the lilac haze of evening. Her imagination could not conceive the silvery crescent of the new moon, or visualise the twinkling candelabra of stars on a frosty night. The trembling hues of a rainbow never excited her sense of beauty, nor the crimson curtain of a Virginia creeper carelessly draped over a cottage gable. Flakes of snow had lightly kissed her cheek and dissolved at its warmth, but she had never been dazzled by its sparkling whiteness reflected in winter sunshine. Indeed she was familiar with the scents and sounds of nature, but a stranger to its manifold forms and figures. And the reader will have inferred the reason. She had been born into a world of darkness; a world which knew nothing of light and luminosity: at least not in the physical sense.

Derby saw its share of the barbarities of which religious intolerance was capable during the unenlightened times of Protestant prejudice and Romanist rule. Within a short space it witnessed four cruel martyrdoms. Joan Waste died during the Catholic reign of Mary, and three priests -- Nicholas Garlick, Robert Ludlam and Richard Sympson -- suffered death during the Protestant rule of Elizabeth. Such martyrdoms have proved victories in the long struggle for freedom of religious opinion and worship; although such methods of persecution were the very antithesis of Christian teaching and remain as nightmares which still haunt our national conscience.

This brief biographical sketch is written without partiality or prejudice. It is not intended to please or offend religious feeling, and is written from the detached and uncontroversial standpoint of the secular historian.

Joan was the twin daughter of William Waste, a barber and ropemaker living in the parish of All Hallows, Derby. Although she lived in a world of darkness, Joan had mastered the art of knitting when she was twelve or fourteen years of age, and became proficient in making hose and sleeves for doublets. Her fingers were seldom idle, for she also helped her father in making ropes.

When her parents died, Joan went to live with her twin brother, Roger, for whom she had a great affection. She early developed a strong religious temperament and daily attended church services during the reign of Edward VI. So great was her devotion to religion that she could find her way unaccompanied to any of the churches in Derby. Like many people afflicted with blindness, Joan was compensated by the possession of a retentive memory, and committed to heart much of what she heard read and expounded from the Bible. Like Mary Jones, the Welsh girl of a later period of history, Joan coveted a Bible and by dint of hard work and self-denial eventually saved up sufficient money to buy a copy of the New Testament. But what, we might ask, was the use of a Bible to one who, even had she possessed the faculty of sight, would not have had sufficient education to read its pages?

But Joan refused to be daunted by her blindness and was in the habit of securing the services of seventy years' old John Hurt, a man of some education who was serving a sentence of imprisonment for debt, and who found relief from the monotony of prison life by reading to his sightless visitor. When sickness or some other inconvenience prevented Hurt from performing this service, Joan enlisted the help of John Pemerton, clerk of the parish of All Saints, who deputised on such occasions. And if he happened to be preoccupied, she applied to several other people to whom she paid a penny or two-pence for the privilege; a payment which entitled her to direct how many chapters they should read, or how many times they should read over the same chapter.

Then, upon the death of Edward and the accession of his sister, Mary, the religious reforms introduced by their father were rescinded and the pre-Reformation faith restored. Along with many others in various parts of the country, Joan refused to abandon her persuasions and was put in prison where she was interrogated by a certain Peter Finch, described as Official of Derby. Her denial of the doctrine of transubstantiation was promptly construed as heresy and she was then summoned to appear before Rafe Baine, Bishop of the diocese, Doctor Draycott, his chancellor, Sir John Port, Henry Vernon, Peter Finch, William Bainbridge and others.

The Articles ministered to her and wherewith she was charged were these:

'First, that she did holde the sacrament of the altar, to be but onlie a memorie or representation of Christe's bodie, and materiall bread and wine, but not his naturall bodie unless it were received, as that it ought not to be reserved from time to time over the altar, but immediatelie to be received, &c.

'Item, That she did holde, in receiving of the sacrament of the altar, she did not receive the same body that was borne of the Virgin Mary, and suffered upon the crosse for our redemption, &c.

'Item, She did holde, that Christ at his last supper, did not blesse the bread that he had then in his handes, but was blessed himself, and by virtue of his wordes of consecration, the substance of the bread and wine is not converted and turned into the substance of the bodie and bloud of Christ.

'Item, She did graunt that she was of the parish of Alhalowes, in Darbie, &c.

'Item, That all and singular the premises are true and notorious by publicke report and fame, &c.'

In defence of these charges, Joan replied to the effect that her beliefs were founded upon Holy Scripture, and upon the teaching of learned men; some of whom were suffering imprisonment and death rather than renounce their convictions. She mentioned a certain Dr. Taylor who had died for conscience' sake, and challenged her examiners 'if they would doe so in like case for their doctrine, which if they would not, she desired them, for God's sake, not to trouble her, being a blinde, poore and unlearned woman, with any further talke, saying (by God's assistance) that she was readie to yeeld up her life in that faith, in such sort as they should appoint.'

This was a courageous statement to make, for many had already perished at the stake for a similar declaration of faith. The Bishop and his Chancellor used various wiles and arguments to try and persuade their prisoner to recant. They contended that Christ was able to make the bread of the sacrament His body as easily as He had turned water into wine, or summoned Lazarus from the tomb. When this approach failed, they began to threaten imprisonment, torture and death until the poor young woman was so bewildered that she appeared to falter in her loyalty. She declared that, if the Bishop would 'take it upon his conscience, that the doctrine which he would have her believe concerning the sacrament was true, and that at the dreadful day of judgment he would answer for her therein, she would then further answer them.'

The Bishop was about to reply in the affirmative, when he was hastily interrupted by the Chancellor who pointed out, 'My Lord, you know not what you do; you may in no case answer for an heretic.'

The Chancellor then turned his attention to the prisoner, asking whether she was prepared to recant or not. Joan replied that if they refused to accept responsibility for the truth of what they would have her believe, then she would answer them no further, and desire them to do their pleasure.

She was then delivered to the bailiffs of the town and imprisoned for a period of four or five weeks until they received a written *De haeretico comubrindo* directing that she be brought to All Saints' Church. Here she was led to the front of the pulpit from which Dr. Draicott delivered a denunciatory sermon in which Joan was accused of denying the doctrine of transubstantiation and in which he alleged that she was not only physically, but spiritually, blind. He further threatened that just as her material body would be shortly consumed by fire, so her soul would be destroyed in hell with everlasting fire. After making further maledictory charges against Joan, the sermon was brought to a conclusion and she was taken to Windmill Pitt where, holding the hand of her brother, she calmly prepared herself for the forthcoming ordeal. She offered several personal prayers, solicited those of the onlookers and 'cried unto Christ to have mercy upon her as long as life served.'

And so, on August 1st, 1556, the sentence of death by burning was carried into effect. While the preparations were being made, Doctor Draicott retired to his inn 'for great sorrow of her death' and there slept through the period of her execution.

Margaret Stafford

'The Lamp of St. Helen'

HANGING in the vestry of Eyam Church is a bronze lamp said to be of Tudor workmanship. It is reputed to be the lamp which stood for many years upon the now vanished altar of St. Helen in the north aisle of the church as a condition of tenure whereby the wealthy Eyam branch of the Stafford family held estates in the district. If this claim is genuine, then it surely must be a replacement of a much earlier lamp, and William Wood (*Tales and Traditions of the Peak*) says that the original lamp stood on the fragment of a coffin lid now built into the north wall of the north aisle. It has been suggested that this stone was actually used as the lamp and that the recessed ornamentation would be filled with oil and contain a floating wick.

Dr. J. C. Cox, the authority on Derbyshire churches, reported failure in his researches to find proof of the existence of this legendary lamp, but the Manuscript Department of the British Museum supplied the required evidence in a 13th century Latin document confirming 'a grant by Eustace de Morteyne of three bovates of land to Richard Stafford to be held by hereditary right, free, undisturbed, and intact wholly and severally in their locality and pertaining to the aforesaid village within and without for the sole purpose of providing one lamp burning before the altar of St. Helen, in the

Church of Eyam, throughout the year while Divine Service is conducted in the said church. This duty frees them from all other duties to me and my heirs.' A further deed conveys the properties to Richard's son, Roger, on the condition stipulated by the father that as 'long as I live I be allowed to exact and demand afterwards the means for performing the duty I have been wont to perform, to wit, to provide one lamp burning before the altar of St. Helen the Virgin, in the Church of Eyam, throughout the year while Divine Service is conducted in the said Church.'

The Chapel of St. Helen is said to have been founded by a member of this ancient family and endowed with a gift of wax to be used in keeping the lamp alight. The chapel was largely occupied by the Stafford-Bradshaw pew, several fragments of which have been adapted, although the artificially constructed hawk-hill remains not far from a tottering fragment of the wing added to Stafford Hall by Francis Bradshaw, grandson of the Francis who had married Ann, one of the daughters of Humphrey, last of the male line. This wing became recognised as Bradshaw Hall and was deserted by members of that family when Eyam was visited by bubonic plague in 1665.

Stafford Hall was described as spacious and massive and had been built in the reign of Henry VI. It is said to have "had narrow windows, black oak floors and a flat roof covered with lead. One very large room had beams upon which family crests were painted, and a fine window filled with tracery. A projecting circular stone in the south wall was carved with the Stafford arms -- a chevron between three martlets. The arms and crest are described in the language of heraldry as follows:- Arms: *Or, a chevron gules, between three martlets sable. Crest: Out of a ducal coronet per pale or and gules, a boar's head and neck sable.*

The two sons of Humphrey Stafford had died before reaching manhood and his four daughters married into influential families, but tradition tells of a fifth daughter, Margaret, who remained single for the purpose of maintaining the lamp in lieu of male descent. The lamp was to be 'superintended by the actual male possesser, or in default of male issue, by female issue during her life on condition of her utterly abstaining from entering into a marriage state or marriage contract. The lands to pass from the family at her death or marriage.' Therefore this mysterious person plays an important role in the apocryphal story concerning the Lamp of St. Helen.

The story dates to the period of Mary Queen of Scot's imprisonment at Chatsworth, when curiosity prompted many local residents to visit that mansion for the purpose of catching a glimpse of the royal captive. At the invitation of his kinsman, the Earl of Shrewsbury, Humphrey Stafford paid a visit to Chatsworth with his daughter, Margaret, and they were privileged with a discreet but favourable view of the royal prisoner. When they returned home after this exciting experience, Miss Staffordshire wrote a letter to an aquaintance, Anthony Babington, who was then in Paris and who had served as one of Mary's pages when she was at Sheffield Castle. She made a number of innocently sympathetic references to the circumstances of the Scottish queen's exile. With womanly compassion, she expressed regret at the indignity of her situation and would welcome improvement in her present status, so long that this would not result in any injury to her royal cousin. Little did she think that these purely personal sentiments, expressed in private correspondence, would one day be interpreted as incriminating evidence sufficient to involve her as party to a conspiracy designed to liberate the royal captive. But the letter, written while her impressions were fresh and vivid, was signed, sealed and despatched by a bearer travelling to the Continent.

Shortly after this memorable visit to Chatsworth, Miss Stafford was taking an accustomed evening stroll in the Delph, a secluded limestone valley south of Eyam. The Delph still remains a haunt of peace and quiet charm, undisturbed by the sounds and scenes of industry; a place where cattle and sheep graze in contentment and where the solitude is unbroken except for the murmur of a stream and the melody of bird song. As she lingered in quiet enjoyment of the scene, her mood of meditation was invaded by a feeling of unease and a sense of some strange supernatural presence. This proved to be a shadowy female figure holding in either hand a lighted lamp. The spectre gave Miss Stafford a message of ill omen concerning her future which she must face alone, warning that at that very moment her father was at the point of death. After delivering her tidings of approaching misfortune, the figure dissolved and, greatly distressed and shaken, Miss Stafford made her way back to the village where she was greeted with news of her father's sudden death.

On the day of the funeral, the black oak coffin studded on the lid with brass nails to form the initials H.S., stood in state in the large tapestried room of the Hall. It was bedecked and surrounded by many floral tokens of affection, sympathy and respect, for the squire had been greatly esteemed in the village and over a wide area. After being conveyed to the churchyard, it was carried once round the ancient Celtic cross; a custom believed to secure the release of the departed soul from purgatory, and then taken into church where the service was conducted by the Rev. Robert Talbot, a friend and frequent visitor at the Hall, who paid tribute to the influence and munificence of the late squire.

Two years later, during mid-August while the Wake was in progress, a stranger presented himself at the Talbot Arms which stood opposite the church. The inn consisted of two ground floor apartments with one large chamber above, and was largely the centre of social activity in the village. Its sign-board was adorned with a painting of a talbot, crest of the Earls of Shrewsbury. The presence of the stranger would normally have attracted attention and speculation, but the inn was crowded with villagers and visitors celebrating the Wake, and so the new arrival excited little interest. He was in a state of agitation and asked for the landlord, Lawrence Decket, who was also a blacksmith, and who, after a brief consultation, left the inn and hurried with the visitor to Stafford Hall where Miss Stafford was on the point of leaving to fulfil her duty of trimming the Lamp of St. Helen.

The stranger produced a letter and hurriedly explained his mission, urging Decket to find some place of hiding for Miss Stafford without delay. Failure to do so, he warned, might result in her arrest and imprisonment on a charge of high treason. The bewildered mistress of the Hall was forthwith taken to the Salt Pan, a deep hidden cleft in the limestone which conveys a stream into the Delph, with the promise that she would be conducted to a more remote and secure hiding-place as soon as circumstances permitted.

The unexpected contents of the letter had filled the recipient with consternation and dismay, for it explained the gravity of her situation and stressed the need for urgent flight to some place of safety. It had been written by Anthony Babington only the day before his arrest at Harrow on a charge of complicity in the plot to release the Scottish exile and restore her sovereignty. While still a fugitive he had recalled that Miss Stafford's letter was probably among a number of Mary's documents which had been seized at Chertsey and examined by Walsingham. In a moment of rashness and ill-judgement, he had passed on this letter to Mary as some assurance of the secret support she might expect, and, as he now feared, this would be brought to the attention of Queen Elizabeth. These conclusions proved to be true and Elizabeth had immediately ordered the apprehension of Stafford and his daughter, unaware, of course, that the father had been dead for the past two years.

The warning letter had been despatched by Babington who had induced the bearer to undertake this dangerous mission with the reward of a purse of gold. The latter, having reached his destination and fulfilled the undertaking, quickly and quietly left the village so as not to arouse suspicion.

About an hour after the temporary concealment of Miss Stafford, four mounted soldiers reached the village and presented themselves at the Hall with a warrant to arrest the master and his daughter. Servants gave them the grudging information that their master was dead and the mistress absent from home. Interrogation failed to reveal the whereabouts of Miss Stafford and, realising that they had been forestalled, the angry soldiers searched the building, cursing the staff for their sullen refusal to inform on their mistress. The next day they searched every house in the village, but still without success and without any encouragement from the householders who resented the intrusion upon their privacy.

Meanwhile, under cover of darkness, Miss Stafford had been conducted to a lonely farm on the edge of the moors not far from the Wet Withins circle. This now ruined farmhouse, the Gotheredge, commanded views in every direction and it was impossible to approach the site without detection. Here she found shelter and warm hospitality at night, often having to seek cover and concealment among the woods and on the moors during the day to evade the vigilance of her persuers. The Hall itself was occupied by the soldiers who scoured the neighbourhood to try and secure the fugitive's arrest. But neither threats of punishment nor attempts at bribery could intimidate, or induce betrayal by, those who knew her secret haunts. Weeks lengthened into months and months into years of unrelaxed, but unrewarded search, yet often, at dead of night, Miss Stafford kept faith with her forefathers by stealing quietly into the silent village church to trim the altar lamp.

With the death of Elizabeth and accession of James, the persecution of Miss Stafford ended and her fortunes were restored under the rule of the new monarch. Her case had been brought to his notice and, as compensation for her sufferings and temporary forfeiture of her estates and privileges, he ordered the annulment of the clause concerning the Lamp of St. Helen as security of tenure. But the stress and strain of continued harassment, and the hardships suffered by one accustomed to social refinements, had told their tale on the worn features of the mistress of Stafford Hall. She resumed the works of charity which had been suspended during her exile and, among, many other generous acts, she is said to have enlarged the church tower and installed the four older bells which it contains. And the lamp still hangs in the church vestry; a visible memorial of this ancient family and the only evidence we can offer in support of this story which centres around the mysterious -- and perhaps mythical -- Margaret Stafford.

Dorothy Mately

'A 17th Century Sapphira'

THE story of Dorothy Mately is epitomised in the parish register of Ashover, near Chesterfield, where her obituary states: *'1660. Dorothy Mately, supposed wife of Jno Flint of this parish, foreswore herselfe, whereupon the ground opened and she sanke over hed Mar 23rd., and, being found dead, she was buried March 25th.'* Crisp and cyptic, this sentence supplies a biography in microcosm. Few more words would be needed to portray her character and she well qualified for recognition in the second category of personalities in that now rare book *Saints and Sinners of Ashover*.

Somewhere on one of the disused lead-mine hillocks of Ashover a wooden tub lies buried in a crater of rocks and sand. The tub was used for 'hotching' minerals; a process of separating lead ore from fluorspar, calcite, barytes and other gangue minerals. Ashover once had several rich mines -- such as Gregory and Overton -- in the limestone zone which forms a geological "inlier" and these provided a prosperous occupation for the inhabitants for many years. An unintended symbol of this ancient industry in the fine lead font is the church which has the distinction of being the only font in Derbyshire moulded with this indigenous metal. Women were formerly employed on surface at the lead-mines, and sometimes in the underground galleries, or 'gates', where they assisted boys who worked as hauliers by the primitive method of being harnessed to tubs or sledges which they dragged from the working face to the shaft bottom.

Dorothy appears to have been an unscrupulous woman whom no one envied or admired: a woman whose moral reputation was such that she has been branded as a '17th century Sapphira.' Her story might well have provided William Hogarth with a further series of caricatures, and it did so impress the imagination of a great contemporary writer, John Bunyan, that he introduced her to the readers of his *Life and Death of Mr. Badman.* Bunyan wrote:

'But above all take that dreadful story of Dorothy Mately, an inhabitant of Ashover, in the county of Derby. This Dorothy Mately, saith the relater, was noted by the people of the town to be a great swearer, and curser, and liar, and thief; just like Mr. Badman; and the labour that she did usually follow was to wash the rubbish that came forth of the lead mines, and there get sparks of lead ore. Her usual way of asserting things was with these kinds of imprecautions, "I would that I might sink into the earth if it be not so," or, "I would God make the earth open and swallow me up."

'Now upon the 23rd March, 1660, this Dorothy was washing ore, upon the top of steep hill, about a quarter of a mile from Ashover, and was there taxed by a lad for taking two single pence out of his pocket, for he had laid his breeches by, and was at work in his drawers; but she violently denied it, wishing that the earth might swallow her up if she had them; she also used the same wicked words on several occasions that day.

'Now, one George Hodgkinson, an Ashover man of good report there, came accidentally by where Dorothy was, and stood awhile to talk with her, as she was washing her ore. There stood also a little child by her tub side, and another a distance from her, calling aloud to her to come away; wherefore the said George took the girl by the hand to lead her away to her that called her; but behold they had not gone above ten yards from Dorothy, but they heard her crying out for help, so looking back he saw the woman, her tub and sieve twirling round, and sinking into the ground.

'Then saith the man, "Pray God to pardon thy sin, for thou art never like to be seen alive any longer."

'So she and her tub twirled round and round till they sank three yards into the earth, and there for a while stayed. Then she called again for help, thinking as she said, she would stay there. Now the man, though greatly amazed, did begin to think which way to help her; but immediately a great stone, which had appeared in the earth, fell upon her head and broke her skull, and then the earth broke in on her, and covered her.

'She was afterwards digged up, and found about four yards within the ground with the boy's two single pence in her pocket, but her tub and sieve could not be found.'

A Tragic Trilogy

Stories of Eyam Plague

OVER three hundred years ago, three women lived in the little village of Eyam, One was a plain, homely type of girl who could knit and sew and mend and bake. The second was a young wife with two small children, mistress of the village rectory and little used to the coarseness of rural society. The third was a farmer's wife; mature and fully occupied with the practical business of bringing up a family of six growing children, in addition to feeding poultry, milking cows, curing bacon, baking bread and making butter and cheese.

None of the three, I am sure, ever dreamed that her name would be remembered centuries later and that she would be memorialised in poems, plays, novels and books concerning Derbyshire history and topography. Not that this would have proved any consolation to them, for, unfortunately, their respective claims to historical recognition were wrought out of the same experience of overwhelming sorrow that suddenly and unexpectedly entered their lives when Eyam was devastated by an outbreak of bubonic plague which reputedly travelled in a bundle of cloth from faraway London. The Rev. E. N. Hoare wrote an epic novel describing the story and giving it the title of *The Brave Men of Eyam*. But this was no reflection on the opposite sex, for the reverend writer would have been the first to acknowledge that the women distinguished themselves with equal courage to the men.

The girl had the unusual christian name of Emmot -- Emmot Syddal. She lived in a thatched cottage which is still standing across from the one where George Viccars, the village tailor, received his treacherous bundle of dress lengths and where the plague began its awful ravages on the 7th September, 1665. The thatch of Emmot's cottage has long been replaced with local slate and the structure has been renovated and restored.

Emmot was one of a family of five daughters and a son. Living so near to the source of infection, it is not surprising that she should have been bereaved of her father, brother and four sisters during the second month of the plague. She and her mother were left to mourn their loss. But there was one person, at least, who shared this crushing blow and to whom she could seek comfort in her grief. This was Towland Torre, her sweetheart. He was son of a flour miller in the neighbouring village of Stoney Middleton, and the two were engaged to be married the following Wakes. In spite of the terrible dangers of infection, Rowland persisted in visiting the stricken village to console his sweetheart. As the number of deaths continued to multiply, Emmot tried to dissuade him from paying his visits, urging upon him the hazards to which he was exposing himself, his family and his neighbours. Eventually the two compromised and agreed to meet whenever possible in a limestone valley not far from the cavern church where services were held after the village church had been closed. This secluded valley, known as Cucklet Delph, provided an admirable trysting-place for the two lovers to meet in quietness and secrecy.

It is at this point that artistic imagination has often taken over to embroider the bare historical facts with garments of fiction. Even William Wood, the local chronicler, failed to resist the temptation to fly the kite of his imagination when relating the incident and describes how Emmot woud shyly retire to the privacy of her bedroom to slip the ring upon her finger in anticipation of her Wakestime wedding.

Novelists have variously ornamented the story with their own ideas of what may have happened in that quiet valley where the voice of the village rector was so often heard as he comforted and counselled his fear-stricken parishioners and urged upon them to remain within the boundaries of the parish. One of the illustrations in *The Brave Men of Eyam* depicts Emmot making a dramatic appeal to Rowland to consider his own safety and that of his neighbours with the cry, 'Rowland! Rowland! come not near me.'

Poets too have seized upon the story and have often idealised the rural romance until the two lovers are transformed into figures cast in the same classical mould as Romeo and Juliet. Their stilted conversation is often concerned with flights of philosophy and the interchange of pious platitudes which would be far above the intelligence of a rustic couple who could neither read nor write, and which would never have entered their heads in their desperate plight. Dramatists have also recognised the possibilities of the story when applied to their particular media, and there has been an increasing accumulation of plays which often highlight the sordid details of the occasion as they have found the physical aspects of the situation an admirable palette upon which to mix the paints of human emotion and passion to colour what might otherwise be a drab plot. Were the young couple tempted to taste the forbidden fruits of their affection? Did they cast aside the restraints of religion? Or did they respect the conventions of morality and accept the counsel and teaching of the Church without question? These are the questions asked and answered in various ways by moulders of the theatrical profession, but we shall never know -- nor would we wish to know -- the real answers.

In the despair of their situation, Rowland no doubt urged the girl to flee the stricken village and here we return to the sober reality of the known facts of history. Emmot had a widowed mother and her loyalties were divided. She probably urged upon the impetuous youth the need for patience; for winter had reduced the monthly totals of death and it was hoped that the severe conditions of frost and snow would stamp out the disease. But with the coming of spring flowers, the threat to life was renewed and on the last day of April, 1666, the name of Emmot was added to the lengthening list of obituaries in the parish register. The girl's mother, unable to endure the loneliness of her empty home, fled to the Delph where she lived in one of the temporary shacks built by fugitives from the village.

Meanwhile, Rowland had continued his visits to the agreed trysting-place but was unrewarded by any glimpse of the girl he loved. His forebodings were confirmed by rumours that Emmot was dead of plague and although he sought out a vantage point above Eyam where he could see the thatched cottage near the church, there was no evidence of life to be seen. No figures entering or leaving; no smoke stealing from the chimney. When the disease had finally spent itself, he was among the first to venture into the desolate village, but, even before he reached the cottage where he had spent so many happy hours, an urchin whom he met in the street had tactlessly broken the news: 'Thy Emmot's dead an' buried i' Cussy Dell.'

Reaching the silent cottage, he found weeds growing at the threshold and between the crevices of the stone-flagged floor. Shutters hung limply from the windows; the door creaked open at his touch; furniture was in disarray; pewter plates, pans and candlesticks were flecked with rust, and the pet linnet lay dead in its wicker cage. ...

Catherine Mompesson was well-bred and genteel. She was a person of delicate health with a deceptive flush upon her cheeks which denoted not the rosiness of vigour and vitality, but an advanced stage of consumption. Pulmonary tuberculosis had been diagnosed by her doctors and this was a complaint for which the then medical profession had no remedy. She had good reason, therefore, when the plague broke out, to plead with her husband to leave the village and seek some place of refuge with her two children, George and Elizabeth.

But her husband, William, while fully aware of the extreme gravity of their situation, was a man with a strict sense of vocation. He had felt called to the ministry of preaching and the prospect of an empty church and vacant pulpit was to him an appalling thought. In their helplessness and distress, the people looked to him for guidance and counsel, and the choice of leaving or staying had to be decided by the arbiter of conscience. Here, again, there was a conflict of loyalties between the family and flock. And he made the decision to stay. Having made this personal resolve, he tried to persuade his young wife to accompany their children to some place of safety. But, although her health was frail, Catherine's will was strong and she refused to yield to his entreaties to consider her own safety. She elected to stay in a rectory made lonely by the absence of childish voices and the patter of infant feet. Her relatives lived far away in County Durham and the few influential friends in the village had no hesitation in packing their belongings and leaving the village with haste as the disease spread from house to house and from one family to another. Among these were the wealthy widow of Squire George Bradshaw and her daughter, Anne. They left the proud mansion on the hillside and never returned to resume occupation.

But Catherine Mompesson stayed on as the carriages of her friends rumbled down the village street. She suppressed any feelings of sadness or longing for her children, in order to support her husband as he consoled the harrassed villagers. Every day was busily occupied with the dispensing of medicines to the sick, making wills for the dying, arranging the provision of food and clothing and carrying out the duties of his calling. He closed the church for worship and the churchyard for funerals, holding services in the cavern eroded from a solitary crag of limestone which has ever since been renowned as Cucklet Church. Once it was thought that the young rector had taken the plague, but fears were allayed by a green discharge from an ulcer in his leg, and his wife rejoiced at his recovery from what she believed to be an attack of the disease. We can well understand her pleasure for it was commonly believed that anyone who survived a mild attack would be immune from further infection.

Whenever the weather was favourable, and the pressure of duty permitted, it was the habit of the rector and his wife to take a walk in the fields behind the rectory with the hope that this exercise might arrest Mrs. Mompesson's illness and fortify her against the plague. One evening in August, as they were taking this accustomed recreation, Mrs. Mompesson paused and suddenly exclaimed: 'Oh! Mompesson! the air, how sweet it smells'.

The heart of the young clergyman turned into ice at the words, for he knew that this wasn't the scent of hay or the fragrance of wayside flowers. His wife had fallen victim to the plague and we now know that the imagined sweetness of the air was due to an increase in blood temperature.

Making an evasive reply, Mompesson suggested that they should retire to the Rectory where his fears were fully confirmed. Mrs. Mompesson soon shared his apprehension as the symptoms developed, but showed the strength of her character by urging her husband not to approach too near lest he should catch the infection. She also apologised to her maid for any harsh rebuke she may have administered during the period spent in her service. As her condition grew worse and the sweating antidotes made her delirious and her conversation at times incoherent, Mompesson chatechised her at intervals from the prayer-book and was convinced by her rational replies that she understood the meaning of the petitions and responses. One sentence was often upon her lips: 'One drop of my Saviour's blood to save my soul from sin.'

Her illness was short, due in part to her physical fraility, and a little while before she died Mompesson enquired how she felt, whereupon she quietly and calmly replied that she was looking for when the good hour should come. After he had offered several prayers to which she responded with clear 'amens', she lapsed into silence and Mompesson asked, 'My dear, dost thou mind?' to which she replied 'Yes', and this was the last word to pass her lips.

His wife's death was a grievous blow to the young clergyman, and the letter he wrote to his orphaned children was couched in pathetic yet brave language as he broke the news of their mother's death, but he continued his duties until the last of the 279 victims had been buried of of a population of just over 300 people. Nor was there any time for relaxation, for he had to supervise the destruction of bedding, clothes and other material which might shelter the germs of plague, and begin the work of rehabilitation. In this work, and all through the time of the Plague, he had received the help and co-operation of his predecessor, the Rev. Thomas Stanley who was one of the ejected clergy of 1662, but who had continued in the village as nonconformist pastor.

Every year, on the last Sunday in August, a bowl of roses is laid on the tombstone of this great and gracious lady who died at the early age of twenty-six and was buried within sight of the rectory which she had occupied for so short and -- towards the end -- so sad a time ...

The third person in this tragic trilogy was Elizabeth Hancock, a woman whose hands were roughened with the work of a busy farming household. Such duties kept her occupied from the dawn hours until the dusk of twilight. Her memorial is a heart-shaped enclosure in the care of the National Trust. It contains seven graves, and in his *Call of England*, H. V. Morton wrote:- 'I think the most touching Plague relic in Eyam is a little cluster of graves in a field some distance from the village. They are protected from wandering cattle by a low stone wall. They are very lonely, with the wind blowing over them, the green moss eating into them, and about them still an air of haste and disaster.'

It was during July of the Plague Year that the neighbouring farmhouse and smithy of the Talbots had been stricken with the silence of loneliness and death, for all the occupants had been buried among the trees of the orchard. The smithy fire was extinguished and the sound of hammer on anvil was heard no more.

Three days after the last of the Talbots had been buried, John and Elizabeth Hancock -- namesakes of their parents -- both complained of the burning sickness and after a few short hours were buried by their mother. She is said to have performed this awful task herself to probably shield her husband and the children from the danger of infection.But the precaution was in vain for, three days later, her husband and two sons, Oner and William, had to be buried in three shallow graves near their former home. And two days later the spade was again required to prepare the grave of Alice and the mother completed her nightmare task the following day by dragging the body of Ann to the last of the moorland graves.

People at Stoney Middleton, a village across the valley, are said to have watched the mourning mother as she dug the graves and dragged the bodies by means of a towel tied round their ankles. Imagination can pay its feeble tribute of sympathy to the bereaved woman, but cannot enter fully into her experience of utter loneliness and despair during that week of cumulative sorrow.

With no relative, friend or neighbour to whom she could turn in her bitterness and anguish, the mother fled from her desolate home to find refuge with an only surviving son who had been apprenticed to the silver trade in Sheffield -- a distance of twelve miles away. Imagination sees the furtive figure stealing under cover of darkness down the rutted road, crossing the Derwent and trudging over the dark moors to reach her destination. Somewhere she had to elude the vigilance of a constable stationed where he might interrogate visiting strangers as to their business, for the Sheffield Constables' Accounts have an entry concerning 'charges about keeping people from Fulwood Spring when the plague was at Eyam.' As far as is known, she remained in the town for the rest of her life.

One of her descendants, incidentally, played a prominent part in the discovery of the art of plating copper with silver, which gave rise to the industry of manufacturing Sheffield Plate. The credit is usually ascribed to his employer, Thomas Bolsouver.

After the farmhouse of the Hancocks had been vacated by the mother, it was never occupied again, the condemned buildings falling into such a state of disrepair that they were demolished. The terraced elevation marking the site can still be traced a little distance from the graves enclosure, and the visitor standing in this hallowed plot of ground may be reminded of the dramatic sentences with which Emily Bronte brought to a close her *Wuthering Heights*. 'I lingered round them, under that benign sky; watched the moths fluttering among the heath and harebells, listened to the soft wind breathing through the grass, and wondered how anyone could ever imagine unquiet slumbers for the sleepers in that quiet earth.'

Although we know nothing of the last days of Mrs. Hancock, we wonder whether she occasionally returned to the little cemetery which will always remain as her memorial. For each summer brings many visitors to this shrine of memories where the sunshine of a happy and contented life was darkened and totally eclipsed by the gloom of death which had brought midnight into the hearts and homes of Rowland Torre, the Rev. William Mompesson and every dweller in the desolated village. In the words of the Quaker poets, William and Mary Howitt:-

And many are the pilgrim feet which tread
Its rocky steeps; which thither yearly go:
Yet less by love of Nature's wonders led,
Than by the memory of a mighty woe,
Which smote, like blasting thunder long ago,
The peopled hills...

Martha Taylor

The Fasting Damsel

WHEREAS the story of Phoebe Bown tells of a fighting woman, that of Martha Taylor concerns a fasting woman. While some characters only figure in the small print of history, Martha at one time looked like making headline material. Living in the remote hamlet of Over Haddon, near Bakewell, she became renowned as the 'Derbyshire Non-such' or, as a more sophisticated writer styled her the 'Mirabile Pecci', because of her prolonged exercise in fasting which excited nationwide interest and curiosity. Both doctors of medicine and doctors of theology travelled long distances -- and journeys were very tedious in the 17th century -- to consult the bed-ridden invalid who lived in this small hamlet. As the period of her fast continued to lengthen, she became more and more the sensation of the century. She was talked about, written about, and even preached about. She had neither publicity manager nor advertising agent, yet her fame spread far and wide.

Some there were who accused the girl of being a fake and a fraud, but could not produce evidence to prove the charge. Others decided that she had discovered some secret of survival without the usual physical sustenance provided by milk, meat, bread, vegetables or fruit. And no doubt there were those who considered that she must be in league with the Devil. The then Earl of Devonshire took so serious a personal interest in the case that he employed physicians and surgeons to examine her, and shared the cost with neighbouring townships of a rota of 40 or 60 women who watched Martha day and night to detect any deceit in her diet. She existed on 'a few drops of stewed prunes, drops of water and sugar, or the juice of a roasted raisin.' A feather dipped in water was used to moisten her lips. Once she inadvertantly swallowed part of a fig and a consequent fit of choking nearly proved fatal.

Martha's illness is said to have been originated in girlhood as the result of a blow on the back struck by an angry neighbour. She had been an invalid since 1662, but began to abstain from solid foods on December 22nd, 1667, when she was eighteen years' old. On one occasion she continued five weeks without sleep, yet her face 'remained fresh and lively, her voice clear and audible, and she was free in discourse.' Her claims to sincerity may be qualified to some extent by her devotion to religion, for her sick-room -- the lower chamber of the cottage in which she lived -- became a preaching-place resorted to by members of different denominations. Sermons were delivered by eminent preachers who may have been more interested in her faith than her fast, and who wished to encourage her developing interest in religious matters. She learned to read and studied various theological works, although it is recorded that 'she pretended to nothing of enthusiasm', but 'attained some knowledge of sacred mysteries.'

Often her room was packed to the point of suffocation and overspill congregations stood in the garden to hear the visiting preachers. A contemporary writer, John Gratton, who was a Quaker living in the neighbouring village of Monyash, casually mentions the fasting damsel in his Journal saying:- 'But sometimes I went two miles to see a woman at Over Haddon who pretended to live without meat; where I met professors (I think I may say) of all sorts. One day a man of London came, called an Independent, and there was a meeting; and having heard of me, desired me to pray before he began to preach.' We note that this worthy Quaker was a little sceptical as to the genuineness of Martha's fast.

Martha survived her fast for some years, although her popularity seems to have waned in the interval between her long illness and her death. She was buried on the 12th June, 1684.

Four different pamphlets were published at the time, copies of two being preserved in the archives of the British Museum. One was written as a sort of scientific thesis by Joseph Reynolds, of King's Norton, who communicated his findings to the Royal Society. Another was written from the theological angle and the last to be printed was published on March 30 1669.

In his *Peak Scenery*, Ebenezer Rhodes mentions what must have been the same person, although he gives a different name:- 'In the year 1667, Bakewell exhibited an imposition very similar in circumstances and duration to the one recently played off by Ann Moore, the fasting woman of Tutbury. Ann Booth, a young maiden of

Bakewell, excited the attention of the public by living without eating or drinking for a space of more than 14 months: during this time she had little sleep, sometimes for 4 or 5 weeks together none at all, and like Ann Moore, of Tutbury, she was diligently watched by physicians and others, who for a long time were unable to detect the imposture.'

Ann Moore, of Tutbury, was a married woman who claimed to have lived without food and drink from 1807 to 1813, and, although watched for sixteen days and nights during the year 1811, escaped detection. She was discovered, however, and exposed as a cheat during a further watch kept from the 21st of April to the 30th of the year 1813, and died a few months later at the age of 53 years. Before she died, she made a confession which was published as follows:-

'Confession of Ann Moore. The Committee who have conducted the investigation of the Case of Ann Moore, after an unremitting and assiduous course of examination, have discovered the Imposture which she so long practised on the public, and think it their duty to publish this her own declaration and confession thereof:

"I, Ann Moore, of Tutbury, humbly asking pardon of all persons whom I have attempted to deceive and impose upon, and above all with the most unfeigned sorrow and contrition imploring the Divine Mercy and Forgiveness of that God whom I have so greatly offended, do most solemnly declare, that I have occasionally taken sustenance for the last six years.

"Witness my hand this Fourth Day of May, 1813.

Her Mark
Ann X Moore

'The above declaration of Ann Moore was made before me one of his Majesty's Justices of the Peace for the County of Stafford.

'Witness to the above Declaration and Signature of my Mother Ann Moore.

Mary Moore

'Signed by order of the Committee, Jos. B. H. Bennett, Secretary.'

Anne Fearne

Married at the 'Miners Arms'

ANNE Fearne, the eighteen years' old daughter of Matthew, keeper of the 17th century Miners' Arms Inn at Eyam, never expected to become mistress of the village rectory, but by the strange dispositon of circumstances she did attain to that station in life. It may equally be said that her husband, the Rev. Joseph Hunt, never expected that his participation in a mock marriage would result in his being able to make the dubious boast that he had been married at the bar of the inn by a lead-miner. But again, by the same twist of events, this was the situation in which he found himself.

Not that the Miners' Arms had any claims to being a 'Gretna Green of the Peak' with some special dispensation for the solemnisation of marriages. Nor had the officiating lead-miner any episcopal authority which would confirm the ceremony as lasting and legal. How then, did it happen?

The Rev. Joseph Hunt was inducted to the living of Eyam in March, 1683, while the Plague was still a vivid memory with many of the villagers. Early during his ministry he was summoned to the Miners' Arms to baptise a sick baby and, after performing this sacrament, was persuaded to join a group of miners drinking in the parlour. Anxious, no doubt, to make a favourable impression on his parishioners, he shared their hospitality not wisely, but rather too well, and became involved in a mock wedding with the landlord's daughter. Sly comments had been made on the comeliness of Anne, and eventually it was proposed that they would make an attractive bridal pair. The young clergyman entered into the spirit of the joke and the ceremony tood place at the bar of the inn. One of the better educated miners stumblingly read the marriage service from the rector's prayer-book and the young couple laughingly made the appropriate responses to the amusement of all concerned.

But the incident had an unexpected and unfortunate sequel. Tongues wagged in the village at the rector's unseemly behaviour, and eventually the scandal reached the ears of the bishop of the diocese who insisted upon the ceremony being legally confirmed. And so, at the altar of the church on the 4th September, 1684, the bizarre joke became actuality, and the young couple were declared man and wife.

But again there was a sequel. The young clergyman was already engaged to a lady of some social status and she promptly sued him for breach of promise. Litigation expenses drained his slender purse, estranged him from many friends and involved him deeply and hopelessly in debt. Because of the pressures brought to bear by the bailiff, and to avoid arrest and imprisonment, he and his young wife had to vacate the rectory and take sanctuary in the church to which a vestry was added to provide them with living accommodation. Here they spent the remainder of their married life, and here their two children, Mary and Sarah, were born and brought up. Thus the ecclesiastical authority, which, by its harsh judgement on an admittedly foolish and misguided action, did make some small atonement by not depriving Hunt of his living and giving him security from those who sought retribution through the remoreseless operations of the law.

During the long winter nights, Hunt -- who was stated to be a capital story-teller -- entertained the village youths with tales of adventure, and found further relief from the monotony of social exile by transcribing the parish register from its commencement in 1630 until May, 1705. Until then these parish records, which included the period of the Plague, had consisted of a loosely assorted collection of manuscripts. The original documents appear to have been lost or destroyed, but the existing register remains as a memorial to the rector and the bride he married at the Miners' Arms. Anne died and was buried in church on December 18th, 1703 while her husband continued his domicile for six more years, dying on December 16th, 1709. He was also buried in church lest his body should be seized in payment of the debt incurred so long ago!

During the early 19th century in the same parish, there was an almost 'carbon copy' of this case. Another clergyman became an innocent fugitive from law. The Rev. and Mrs. Charles Hargrave settled into Eyam Rectory secure in the knowledge that the living had been duly purchased by a wealthy aunt for the sum of £2,000. In those days the benefice of Eyam was greatly coveted because of its implementation by revenues derived from lead tithes which increased the annual value from a modest £130 to £1,600 per year at the peak of prosperity.

Then came a shock. The rector's aunt had died and also the titled lady from whom it had hitherto been assumed that she had purchased the living. The young duke who had inherited the estates promptly applied to the rector for immediate payment of the alleged outstanding purchase money. Frantic search of papers belonging to the deceased aunt revealed neither correspondence nor receipts to prove payment. The clergyman's plight was desperate for he now had a family of three children and his financial situation had been seriously impaired by a rapid decline in lead-mining prosperity.

Meanwhile, the duke's impatience was growing and protests that the premium had been duly paid were bluntly repudiated. Bailiffs were sent to arrest the rector who, at a hurriedly convened meeting, frankly explained the situation to his sympathetic parishioners. They expressed willingness to thwart the mission of the bailiffs and for five years co-operated in frustrating attempts to take the rector into custody. Sometimes, he was hidden for days among the winding passages of a cavern which penetrates the limestone south of the village, being faithfully supplied with provisions by the faithful villagers. A lingering tradition still claims that there is a secret passage connecting the rectory with the cavern.

The movements of Hargrave were shrouded in mystery, and the bailiffs -- unable to achieve their objective by bribery, threats or persuasion -- left the vilage. But the duke was still determined to exact vengeance and employed the services of two famous Bow Street detectives named Digby and Brownlow. They had achieved a considerable reputation in the field of crime detection, and were quite confident of success in apprehending a country parson. Before leaving London on this assignment, they had made themselves as familiar as possible with the habits and movements of the rector. Arriving under cover of darkness, they entered the churchyard with stealth and began to keep vigil among the graves and headstones, with the intention of pouncing upon their unsuspecting victim the next morning.

As they sat in the quiet churchyard, so far away from the business and bustle of London, the two men were conscious of a sense of eeriness; more so when they discerned the misty figure of a woman plodding over the graves, muttering and moaning to herself. Cold shivers trickled down their spines and each tongue was parched and dry as the figure halted and cried with a tremulous voice: 'Robert! Come forth. Robert! Come forth.'

Springing to their feet, the two officers ran stumbling over the grassy mounds, out of the churchyard and away from the village. Nor did they return. Nor did the rector suffer further molestation. And all because a poor, deranged widow made pilgramage to the churchyard to summon her long-dead husband from the peace of his grave.

Hannah Baddaley

Of 'Lover's Leap' Fame

WHEN asked by members of the village Women's Institute to devise a competition consisting of the jumbled names of some Derbyshire personalities, I produced a selection of such names along with clues intended to assist in their identification. For example:- MADE THIDE LISTEWL (Rings on her fingers and bells on her prose), CELORFEN ELATINGNIGH (Didn't sing in Berkeley Square) and REGGOE NONSHESTEP (His sputnick never reached the moon).

The competition proved quite a success and there was keen rivalry to rearrange the letters in correct and intelligable order. But one name, although elucidated, provided something of a mystery. It was the name of Hannah Baddaley, and the clue: She didn't jump for joy.' Who, it was asked, was Hannah Baddaley? What claims had she to prominence in county history? And why didn't she jump for joy? Although the name did not provoke a responsive echo, the action which resulted in her notoriety did, for she was the jilted maiden who, goaded on by disappointment and unrequited love, parachuted one day into Stoney Middleton Dale and created the living legend of the Lover's Leap.

'Oh! I see,' light dawned upon the enquirers, 'that was her name -- Hannah Baddaley.'

The landmark associated with Hannah's name is a limestone precipice at the entrance to Stoney Middleton Dale, and far outweighs in interest the rival leaps at Buxton, Matlock and Dovedale which have long since lost their magic and remain as monuments to forgotten romances. The grey rocks towering above the former Lover's Leap Inn (now a transport cafe) are speckled each springtime with gold and orange coloured velvet of wild gilliflowers which have colonised the area for centuries. Robert Murray Gilchrist had a particular affection for this variety of rock plant, and took every opportunity to introduce them to his readers.

Hannah had for some time been the proud recipient of the advances of a youth named William Barnsley, and the two were obviously much infatuated with each other. The romance prospered and the couple basked in the sunshine of each other's affection. Then, sad to say, the sweetness of their love turned sour. Honey became gall. Heaven turned into hell. The blossoms of springtime changed with nightmare swiftness into the sere and blighted leaves of winter. The song of the skylark became the harsh croak of the carrion crow. What had been a sun-drenched landscape was suddenly shrivelled into a bleak and blasted region of despair.

History is silent as the the reason for this cruel caprice, but we assume that it was William's ardour which had grown listless and cool. We suspect it may have been some charming rival who had supplanted Hannah in his affection; or it may have been some quarrel which created the wound that would not heal in her heart. Whatever the reason, it was the love of Hannah which had been so cruelly spurned and rejected. She felt that she could no longer face her family and friends. Sympathy was not a sufficient salve to soothe her sorrow and memories of happier days haunted her and only served to mock and increase her misery. The more she pondered upon the past, the more unendurable became the present; producing in her a mood of moroseness and melancholy for which there seemed to be neither medicine nor healing remedy.

So, after grieving for some while over her slighted affections, Hannah decided upon the most desperate of all expedients to solve her problem; that of suicide. Whether it was a sudden impulse or a premeditated decision we do not know. The only positive record we have is that, about the year 1762, the disconsolate maiden left her home on an undisclosed mission. With unsmiling eyes, firmly compressed lips and an unwavering determination she climbed the steep slopes of the common land west of the village. Here the uptilted limestone strata has been split open by primeval forces and the cleavage of rocks has resulted in the abrupt cliffs which form the northern 'cheek' of Stoney Middleton Dale.

Reaching the highest point overlooking the village, tradition tells that Hannah laid her bonnet and scarf and gloves on the grass at the edge of the cliff and made a melodramatic speech in which she absolved William from responsibility for her death and then jumped into space. She was wearing a crinoline dress and, instead of plunging to the ground, her skirts billowed out to form a parachute, thus arresting her headlong descent. Brambles growing on the ledges of rock snatched at her garments and further impeded her fall until she rolled into a dry sawpit at the base of the cliff.

Witnesses of the incident hastened fearfully to the scene, fully expecting that the fall had been fatal, but, although the girl was unconscious and bleeding from her injuries, she was carried home and nursed back to health again. When she was fully recovered, it became obvious that the physical shock had proved an effective cure for the psychological and emotional condition which had resulted from her experience of frustrated love, and she spent the remainder of her life in single estate. Whether her injuries did anything to curtail her life, we are not told, but she did not live long enough to become bent with the burden of many years, dying at the age of twenty-six.

The records of Hannah's baptism ('Hannah Baddaley, daughter of William and Joan Baddaley, baptised February 22, 1738') and her obituary ('Hannah Baddaley, buried December 12') remain in the parish register, but the site of her grave in Stoney Middleton churchyard cannot now be identified. It was marked by a headstone of local sandstone, the surface of which has peeled away as the result of erosion, carrying with it the inscription. At her death she left a modest fortune of £180.

Hannah's story has been compared with one told by Sappho, a lyric poetess of Greece who was living in 611-592 B.C. She described the experiences of a jilted girl in a romantic story entitled *Unrequited Love* and this exercise in prose has proved more popular and enduring than her works of poetry. And so Sappho and Phaon have become renowned in classical legend and literature as prototypes of ruptured romance, but in Derbyshire history and folk-lore such roles will ever be filled by the perfidious William and his hapless victim -- Hannah.

Jedediah Buxton

The Mathematical Marvel

ONE day in 1772 a local labourer called on the Duke of Portland at Welbeck Abbey with a request to see his Grace. The matter was one of urgency for, the caller confided to the butler who answered his summons, 'I shall never see his Grace again.' The puzzled nobleman asked the equally puzzled butler to show in the caller and enquired the reason for the interview. He was solemnly informed: 'I am come to thank your Grace for all the favours you have bestowed upon me, for I shall never see your Grace any more.'

When the Duke asked the reason for such a strange declaration, his visitor reiterated: 'I must never see you again; I must come here again no more.'

'But why, Jeddy?' asked the Duke.

'Because I shall die next Thursday.'

During the ensuing conversation, the Duke tried to persuade Jeddy that perhaps he wasn't feeling well, or was suffering from some temporary delusion, and quietly instructed the servants not to give him much beer 'for the old man's brain grows weak.' The servants were quite amused at the old man's prophecy and the seriousness with which it was asserted.

But neither laughter nor levity prevailed to change Jeddy's belief and he spent the intervening days taking leave of his friends, none of whom believed that he was in earnest or in his right mind.

Thursday arrived. Jeddy discharged his normal duties, ate his dinner, then sat down and died, greatly to the astonishment of those who had ridiculed his prophecy.

This singular story was one singular incident in the life of a singular man. Jedediah Buxton was born at Elmton on March 20th, 1707, and died there on March 5th, 1772. Son of the village schoolmaster, William Buxton, and grandson of a vicar, the Rev. John Buxton, Jedediah was described as a stupid boy, never learning to read and write and spending his working career as a labourer. But he had a natural endowment which matched that mechanical miracle of human ingenuity and invention so indispensible to modern life -- the calculator. His only educational achievement in this direction was to learn the multiplication table as a youth, and henceforward mental arithmetic became his sole passion. He had the remarkable facility to tackle a complicated series of figures and, in the midst of the exercise, break off and resume the calculation after a considerable lapse of time. Sometimes he would invite two people to pose a different problem in succession to each other, providing them with their respective answers and, if required, repeating them after the passage of one or two months. But apart from this facility for figures, his mental age was said to be only ten when he reached manhood.

Here are some of the problems he was asked to solve.

Admit a field to be 423 yards long and 383 wide, what would be the area? After the figures had been clearly repeated to him, he gave the correct product of 162,009 yards in the space of two minutes. How many acres would the aforesaid field measure? In eleven minutes he arrived at the answer of 33 acres, 1 rood, 35 perches and 20¼ yards. Asked how many times a coach wheel of 6ft. diameter would revolve in travelling the 204 miles between London and York, he produced the answer in one and a half minutes. It took him the same time to calculate that 1,520,640 barley corns would reach a distance of eight miles. Asked what would be the sum computed by 140 nails being doubled at a farthing a nail, he reached the answer of £725,958,238,096,074,907,868,531,656,993,638,851, 106 - 2s. - 8d. He then went on to multiply this figure by itself! Another similar feat of rapid reckoning was to calculate the product of a farthing doubled 139 times, the answer to which the reader might care to figure out whithout the resources of a ready reckoner.

His severest test took over a month to complete, and Jedediah confessed that it 'made him drunk wi' reckoning' and that he must have a good sleep to restore him to sobriety. The problem posed was: How many hairs one inch in length, and how many grains of eight different kinds of corn and pulse would reach two hundered miles? Jedediah adopted the measure of 48 hairs to an inch, and this corresponds with that of the Jewish standard of measurement relating to a hair's breadth.

He was asked by his employer, Sir John Rodes, of Barlborough Hall, to furnish him with the measurements of his estate, and this he did by pacing out the areas of pasture, plough and wood land, providing the result in acres, roods and perches with the accuracy of a professional surveyor.

A contributor to the *Gentleman's Magazine,* writing under a possible pseudonym of George Saxe of Sherwood Forest, drew attention to this genius who 'without the assistance of pen, ink or chalk, will multiply four or six figures by as many, or divide large sums off-hand sooner than the most precise of your mathematicians pretend to.' Buxton was gifted in that 'without being able to write or cast Accounts in the Ordinary method perform'd the longest Calculations and solv'd the most difficult Problems in Arithmetic by the strength of his Memory.' The letter of Saxe was not designed solely to draw attention to Buxton's remarkable qualifications in the science of mathematics, but to bring to the notice of the public his impoverished state. 'The motive inducing me to write this is to rescue this poor and obscure man from oblivion desiring to see his name in your far and near travelling Magazine that the whole world may know and assist if they please this surprising genius now cloathed in rags, and labouring hard with his spade for the support of himself and a large family.' If such a worthy advocate as the writer had been prepared to act as manager to sponsor Jedediah on the stage, his talented performances before the public might have lifted him from such a sad situation, but Saxe appears to have been satisfied in commending him to the charity and benevolence of readers of the magazine.

George Saxe reported a personal interview with Buxton. 'I met him by chance last summer and after hearing of his performances I first proposed to him the following random question: In a body whose three sides are 23,145,789 yards and 5,642,732 yards, how many cubical ½'s of an inch? After once naming the several figures distinctly one after another, in order to assure himself of the several dimensions and fix them in his mind, without more ado, he fell to work amidst more than one hundred of his fellow labourers, and after leaving him about five hours, on some necessary concerns (in which time I calculated it with my pen) he told me he was ready; upon which he asked me which end I would begin at, for he would direct me either way. I chose the regular method, and to my great surprise found that in a line of 28 figures he made no hesitation nor the least mistake.'

Buxton devised his own mathematical terminology, referring to the cube of a million as a 'tribe', and a thousand tribes of tribes as a 'cramp'. The following example is given of his method of calculation.

Asked to multiply 456 by 378 he worked in the following cumbersome stages:

1st step: 456 x 5 = 2,280
2nd step: 2,280 x 20 = 45,600
3rd step: 45,600 x 3 = 136,800, i.e. the product of 456 x 300
4th step: 2,280 x 15 = 34,200 i.e. product of 456 x 75
5th step: 136,800 + 34,200 = 171,000
6th step: 456 x 3 = 1,368
7th step: 171,000 x 1,368 = 172,368

He was interested in figures to the exclusion of all other academic interests or pursuits. When attending a performance by David Garrick of Richard III at Drury Lane Theatre, the quality of acting and the eloquence of the language left him quite unimpressed, for he had spent the evening counting the number of words spoken by the great actor. The magic and mystery of figures was more important to him than that of words! When he attended church, which was his regular custom, he could not remember the text, let alone the substance of the sermon.

An outstanding adventure was his journey on foot to London early in 1754 and he was depicted in the *Gentleman's Magazine* with wide-awake hat and staff in hand making his pilgrimage to the metropolis. His stay of several weeks was made possible by the patronage of several acquaintances, and it was during this occasion that he made his rather unresponsive visit to the theatre. He stayed at St. John's Gate and was bitterly disappointed that his ambition to see the royal family was unfulfilled, for George II was away at Kensington Palace at the time. He was less fortunate than Samuel Slack, Derbyshire's famous singer, who was invited to give a command performance before George III at Windsor Castle.

But on the 25th April he was somewhat compensated by an invitation to demonstrate his prowess before members of the Royal Society who were quite impressed by his mental agility with figures, and the following record was entered in the proceedings of this august assembly:- 'The Society being informed that Jedediah Buxton, a Man who had an extraordinary Memory, and could perform several Operations by his head, Attending without, He was called in, and performed Some Such operations, particularly Multiplying four Figures by four Figures, the telling the Changes in a number of Bells, and the Extraction of the Square Root of a Number which last he Said he had never performed before.

'For which a Small Gratuity, was ordered to be given to him.'

But Jedediah's fame never brought him fortune. After his stay in London, he trudged back to his native Elmton to resume his work as a manual labourer. His portrait was painted in January, 1764, by Miss Hartley, and this was later engraved. As may be imagined, Jedediah couldn't be guilty of wasting time just 'sitting' for the portrait, so he occupied himself in calculating how many seconds he had lived from the time of his birth to that particular moment in time. He arrived at the conclusion that he had existed for 1,792,230,823 seconds! He was also able to state how many 'winds', or pints, of beer he had consumed since reaching the age of twelve. No stone was ever placed in the churchyard to mark Jedediah's grave, but his portrait hangs in the church vestry to remind the present generation of its 18th century celebrity.

James Brindley

The Canal Engineer

'THE English are a dumb people. They can do great acts but not describe them. Whatsoever of strength the man had in him will be written in the work he does. The rugged Brindley has little to say for himself. He has chained seas together. His ships do visibly float over valleys, and invisibly through the hearts of mountains; the Mersey and the Thames, the Humber and the Severn, have shaken hands.'

These words were written by John Ruskin as testimony to James Brindley, a pioneer of canal transport who was born in 1716 in the parish of Wormhill. In the centre of the village is a hollow where a triangular stone canopy covers a well and bears the inscription: '1875. In memory of James Brindley, canal engineer, born in this parish, A.D. 1716.' This memorial was described by J.B. Firth (*Highways and Byways of Derbyshire*) as 'an ugly affair, hopelessly inartistic and crude', but it was Wormhill's sincere and genuine tribute to its greatest celebrity; the man who helped to create a new dimension in industrial transport.

For many years an ash tree marked the site of the cottage at Tunstead where this illiterate genius was born. It was locally known as Brindley's Tree, having grown from a seedling which lodged between a crevice of the paving stones of the ruined cottage. Stone was pilfered from the ruin, and so were the wooden beams and rafters, but, when all trace of the building had disappeared, Brindley's Tree remained as self appointed guardian of the site, and when this tree fell victim to time the Derbyshire Archaeological Society planted a sapling to carry on the tradition.

Brindley was the son of a farm labourer who had no means to afford money for his son's education, and when only a child he was employed scaring birds from fields where crops had been sown. Later, he drove wagons conveying corn to the local mill and here the grinding processes roused his instinct for engineering. He made models of the machinery and set them to work in streams devised from the overflow of stone troughs. His lack of education proved no deterrent to his determination to make progress in some sphere of engineering, and, at the age of seventeen, he did like William Newton, the poetical carpenter, and forsook the fields and farms of Tunstead, becoming apprenticed to Abraham Bennett, a mill-wright at Sutton, near Macclesfield.

The following period enlarged his knowledge and experience as he carried out his duties as journeyman engaged in the fitting or repair of the machinery of various mills. His work in repairing machinery damaged or destroyed by a fire at a Macclesfield mill was of such a high standard that he earned the commendation of the mill-owner and was encouraged to undertake designs for machinery at a new paper mill. When Brindley was twenty-one years' old, his master was so impressed by the quality of his workmanship and his understanding of the technicalities involved, that he put him in charge of his workshop. But Bennett's death in 1742 terminated his apprenticeship and he became established as a self-employed engineer and mill-wright at Leek where his business prospered and he began to employ labour to meet increasing demands for his services. During these days he earned the nickname of 'The Schemer.'

Another development in his engineering activities was to devise and fabricate methods of pumping to de-water coal-mines subject to flooding problems. The design of steam engines also began to engage his attention. His reputation was becoming known to prominent figures in the industrial world, including Josiah Wedgwood. In 1755 he was employed in the erection of a silk mill at Congleton, but was restricted to the larger wheels and coarser apparatus, another engineer being entrusted with the more refined and delicate work, and also having supervision over the whole operation. But the superior knowledge and workmanship of Brindley asserted itself and, after having been obliged to correct some of the faulty work of his senior, he was entrusted with completion of the entire work. One of his inventions at this time was a system of cutting tooth and pinion wheels by machinery and this was more effective than the existing method carried out by hand.

Brindley's great opportunity came when he was invited to advise the Duke of Bridgwater on a scheme for providing a canal to convey coal from his estate at Worsley to Manchester -- a distance of 10½ miles. The Duke's father had obtained an act in 1732 for such a venture, but the scheme had failed due to the enormous cost. One of the greatest difficulties to be surmounted was that of crossing the Irwell at Barton, and, although he had no technical knowledge of the science of surveying, the enthusiastic Brindley assured the Duke that this presented no problem to his carrying out the scheme. He suggested a second opinion and a consultant engineer accompanied Brindley to the site where he explained his idea for an aqueduct. The sceptical engineer was so unconvinced of its practicality that he scathingly remarked that he 'had often heard of castles being built in the air, but had never before been shown where any of them were to be erected.' But the Duke was convinced that his confidence in Brindley was not misplaced and decided to proceed with the venture. The aqueduct was nine hundred yards long, seventeen feet high, and supported by three massive stone arches with embankments at each end. The work began in September, 1760, and was completed in July of the following year, and, as a result of the economy in transport costs, the price of coal was reduced in Manchester from 7d. to 3½d. per cwt. A writer in the *Annual Register* for 1763 described the Barton Aquduct saying that while he was 'surveying it with a mixture of wonder and delight, four barges passed in the space of three minutes, two of them being chained together and dragged by two horses, who went on the terras of the canal, whereon I must own I hardly dare venture to walk, as I almost trembled to behold the large river Irwell underneath me.'

Brindley travelled hundreds of miles on horseback to visit the site of his engineering labours, rather like his contemporary, John Wesley, but preaching another gospel. He spent himself unsparingly, tirelessly advocating the value of water in industry as a means of communication and power. Sometimes, when confronted by a particularly difficult problem, he would retire to bed for several days until he had found a solution. His natural aptitude for engineering was such that, after careful observation of its mechanism and principle of working, he could construct an exact copy of a machine.

His second major achievement was the construction of the twenty-four miles' long Manchester-Liverpool Canal for the Duke of Bridgwater. He designed a special barge at this time to carry cargoes of excavated material to be deposited at required sites by means of a hinged bottom. Brindley was paid the none too generous salary of one guinea per week for his skill and expertise, while the army of five hundred labourers received 1s. 2d. per day. The cost of the two canals totalled £220,000, but the resulting revenues exceeded this initial expenditure in three years. Before this project was finally completed, the indefatigable Brindley was planning an even more ambitious work. This was the Grand Trunk Canal to which Ruskin referred, and this linked Liverpool, Hull and Bristol by navigable waterways. For this enterprise, Brindley received financial sponsorship from Wedgwood who recognised the potential to industry of such an undertaking. This system took eleven years to accomplish, involving the construction of five tunnels and about three hundred aqueducts. It was one of the wonders of the world of engineering.

On one of his visits to London to supply evidence in support of the Duke's Bill before Parliament, Brindley -- like Jedediah Buxton --

paid a call at the Drury Lane Theatre to see Garrick's performance of Richard III. This was his first and only visit to the theatre, for his mental reactions to the great actor's performance were so stimulated that he could think of nothing else for the next two days, and he determined never to visit such a place again. While in London, he purchased a pair of shoes and several garments, making a note that the 'now shoos' had cost him 6s., and 'now briches' a guinea. He also recorded the results of the division in Parliament in favour of the Duke's Bill:- 'ad a grate Division of 127 fort Duk. 98 nos. for te Duk 29 Me Jorete.'

At the age of fifty, Brindley married Anne Henshall who was thirty years his junior, and they lived at Turnhurst, near Harecastle. He still continued his work of harnessing water for barge transport, constructing the Birmingham Canal in 1768 and another at Droitwich. While surveying a canal near Leek, he was drenched by a downpour of rain, but was too preoccupied to change his wet clothes. A resulting illness developed into diabetes and, at the age of fifty-six, he died on September 27th, 1772, and left behind, as his memorial, about 250 miles of inland waterways as well as the 'ugly affair, hopelessly inartistic and crude', where the people of Wormhill erect their floral tableau for the annual festival of well-dressing.

John Whitehurst

Clockmaker and Geologist

I HAVE always coveted a clock or barometer made by John Whitehurst of Derby. Once I saw a Whitehurst weatherglass in a London antique shop, but it bore no advertised price and I must confess that I am a little suspicious of unpriced articles. Moreover, from the inscribed date it was a product of the third John Whitehurst and not of his uncle, so I did not overcome my scruples and enquire the price.

The famous John Whitehurst was born on April 10th, 1713, son of John Whitehurst, a clockmaker of Congleton in Cheshire. Not much is known of his early career, except that he had a rather indifferent education, but developed an interest in the geological structure of north-western Derbyshire while still a youth. He established himself in business as a clockmaker at 22 Irongate, Derby, in 1736. Two years before settling in Derby, John is said to have visited Dublin with the intention of elucidating the secret of a curious clock in that city.

But the owner was jealous of his rare possession, denying access to the clock and thwarting any attempts at infringement of patent by keeping it securely under lock and key. John, however, was not so easily frustrated in his quest and, by obtaining lodgings in the same premises, he contrived by stealth to discover the secret of its mechanism.

The rate of business success in his new environment was slow at first, but John prospered after achieving the status of burgess as reward for making and installing a public clock in the newly erected Town Hall. His reputation spread to various parts of the Midlands where his clocks had become noted for reliability and were being installed in churches, mansions and public buildings. For a period he was also a churchwarden at All Saints' Church.

In an interesting tract published by the Local History Section of the county's archaeological society, Mr. W.D.White wrote:- 'In his turret clocks he fitted pendulums of both seconds and longer intervals. All pendulums had lenticular bobs. The majority of the escapements were "recoil" but beautifully made and closely fitted. His best clocks were "dead-beat" of the pin-wheel type; the invention of the pin-wheel is often ascribed to him, but the actual originator was the Frenchman "Amant". However, John Whitehurst was one of the first makers to adopt it for large public clocks. He did not protect any of his innovations and no patent application for clocks is filed at the Patent's Office under the name of Whitehurst.

'He invented a tell-tale clock which was widely used in mills to check the night watchman. The system was adopted by the Derby police and was in use as late as 1860. These clocks have narrow oak cases and both 12 and 24 hour rotating dials were fitted. A protruding peg, placed each half hour interval, passed under a plunger, which when depressed drove in the peg and so recorded the watchman's vigilance. The pegs were automatically returned to their normal position at a later hour. With a set of these clocks, a finely made 3 train 8 day ting tang ¼ clock was installed to regulate them by. He also put on the market a clockwork egg-timer with unsprung verge escapement. The principle employed anticipated the modern mechanical egg-timer.'

Whitehurst formed a friendship with James Ferguson F.R.S., the astronomer and instrument maker, who lectured at Derby in 1762 and 1775, and the two maintained a correspondence until Ferguson's death in 1776. Another personal acquaintance was his fellow citizen, Joseph Wright, the artist, who wrote to a friend shortly after his return from Italy: 'Remember me with respect to all my friends: when you see Whitehurst tell him I wished for his company on Mount Vesuvius, his thoughts would have centered in the bowels of the mountain, mine skimmed over the surface only. There was a considerable eruption at the time of which I am going to make a picture.'

And it was probably with this vivid memory in mind that the artist, when painting a portrait of Whitehurst, depicted him against a background of Vesuvius in eruption. In this picture the subject is represented examining a parchment inscribed 'A Section of the Strata of High Tor.'

When the Government established the office of 'Stamper of Money Weights' in 1775 to secure the standard of gold currency, the Duke of Newcastle -- for whom Whitehurst had made the clock at Clumber Park -- recommended the Derby clockmaker for the position and he was appointed. This entailed his removal to London and he took up residence at 4 Bolt Cort, Fleet Street, where his former friend Ferguson had lived and died. It had also been the home of Dr. Johnson. This change resulted in a new phase in his career, and he turned his attention to literary and scientific pursuits and to a variety of theoretical exercises and practical experiments. He produced a thesis entitled 'Observations on the Ventilating of Rooms' and the system he advocated was applied to the wards of St. Thomas' Hospital, London, while his 'garden stoves' were used at Kedleston Hall to create temperatures favourable to the growing of pines, and the Duke of Newcastle employed him to supply heating for his greenhouses at Syon House. In similar vein he attempted to diagnose and effect 'The Cure of Smoky Chimneys', using an experimental fireplace which consumed two hundredweights of coal in twelve hours. Had the experiments proved successful, he would no doubt have been rewarded by a fortune, but the problem was not confined to a regular pattern and had many complexities, being influenced by type of premises, situation, weather and other contributory conditions. William Hutton, the Derby historian, commented with tongue in cheek:- 'Smoaky Chimnies: an evil under which half the world groans. And which every petty builder can cure, but still the evil remains, if it should ever be removed, it must be by a Whitehurst.'

One of his philosophical exercises was entitled 'An Attempt towards Invariable Measures of Length, Capacity and Weight from the Mensuration of Time', but the work of particular interest to Derbyshire was his 'Inquiry into the Original State and Formation of the Earth'. He became a Fellow of the Royal Society in 1779. While paying a visit to the Giant's Causeway during the summer of 1783,

Opposite:- Top: Left, Jedediah Buxton; Right, James Brindley. Bottom: Left, John Whitehurst; Right, Joseph Wright.

he constructed an engine required for pumping water from a well to the summit of a hill in a bleaching ground in County Tyrone.

Whitehurst married in 1745 the daughter of the Rev. J. Gretton, Rector of Trusley and Dalby, but their only child died in infancy. His business was continued by his nephew and heir, John, son of James Whitehurst who had remained at Congleton in his father's business. One of his contemporaries, the historian Hutton, refers to his casual meeting with Whitehurst: 'I saw him at Buxton in 1785 and wished his acquaintance. He was near six feet high, straight, thin, and wore his own dark-grey bushy hair; he was plain in his dress, and had much the appearance of a respectable farmer.' Whitehurst died on the 18th February, 1788, and was buried in St. Andrew's churchyard in Gray's Inn Lane where his wife had been buried in November, 1784.

The craftsman has long been dead, but many of his clocks still patiently tick away the seconds, minutes and hours for the benefit of this present generation, and his barometers predict the weather as the seasons come and go. Not many students of geology consult his rather quaint 'Inquiry' as a technical or scientific text-book, but we must acknowledge him as a pioneer of the then primitive science of geology. His contention that toadstone was of volcanic origin was violently disputed by some contemporary geologists, but his theory has been proved to be correct. William Wood wrote:- 'The indefatigable Whitehurst contended that this stratum was of igneous origin; and he supported his darling supposition with unabating zeal. St. Fond, a French geologist, came into Derbyshire a little after Whitehurst's time to examine this formation in particular; he descended Dirtlow Mine, near Castleton, and on beholding mineral in composition with the toadstone he almost shouted with exultation, it being his particular object to disprove Whitehurst's theory. St. Fond sums up his observations by expressing great wonder that Whitehurst could have been so fatally mistaken as to perceive proofs of his igneous theory where evidently everything is of aqueous origin. After much conflict of opinion on this subject -- the igneous or the aqueous origin of toadstone -- the balance is greatly in favour of the latter theory.' But it has long been proved that St. Fond, Wood and all who subscribed to their belief, were the ones in error and not Whitehurst and his supporters. He was equally cautious in his attempts to discover the cause of explosions due to 'slickensides', describing it as a phenomenon when others claimed it to be a mineral distinct from galena.

The epitaph composed for an 18 years' old Bolsover craftman might have been suitable for Whitehurst, for it states that 'Here lies in a horizontal position the outside case of Thomas Hinde, Clock and Watch maker, who departed this life wound up in hope of being taken in hand by his Maker and being thoroughly cleaned, repaired and set a-going in the world to come.'

Penelope Boothby

'The Mob Cap'

MANY years ago I saw a parchment-coloured copy of a slender book of verse in a second-hand bookshop in Nottingham. Its jaundiced appearance was due to age and it was tucked in an obscure corner of a top shelf in the basement. It was entitled *Sorrows Sacred to Penelope* and was priced one guinea. Folio in size, it had a frontispiece engraving illustrating the triumph of Love over Death, which, I learned later, was the work of an artist named Fuseli. I fondled the book and pondered the price. In those days a guinea represented nearly half a week's wage, and I had a wife and small family to consider. So, with reluctance, I returned it to the shelf and have never since seen a copy of the work.

But I have always had an affection for Penelope. Whenever I visit Ashbourne Church I pay my respects in the little chapel where she sleeps in calm repose; her body relaxed, her features composed, her garment falling in graceful pleats and folds, her hands clasped and her cheek resting on the marble pillow. She reminds me of a Sleeping Beauty waiting for the awakening kiss of some fairytale prince.

In another work I have written that 'there are few children who have brought so much sunshine into life, and left it -- after a handful of short years -- with so much shadow. The sculptor has successfully imbued the reclining figure with a suggestion of tenderness and innocent charm, and the attitude of relaxation hints at the peace which follows pain... She lies upon her mattress cold and still; deaf to the cadences of Ashbourne's bells; blind to the gaze of tourist, and mute in her appeal to their sympathy and emotions; a little girl who unconsciously enriched art and made her name immortal.'

The art of the sculptor never fails to excite my wonder and admiration. With other artistic skills, it is often a simple matter to correct a mistake, but not so with mallet and chisel. A flaw in the stone or a moment's lack of concentration may cause irreparable damage, or put at risk the results of hours of painstaking labour. And this figure of Penelope wrought by Thomas Banks, R.A., intrigues and fascinates me by its perfection of detail, and will long keep alive the memory of its creator when his other works are virtually forgotten.

This monument reminds me of the little known figures of a sleeping mother and child in Rowsley Church. In a specially dedicated chapel is the sleeping figure of 23 years' old Catherine, wife of Lord John Manners who became the 7th Duke of Rutland. Wearing a simple gown she lies with hands folded upon her breast, while, lying on the mattress at her side and sharing her tranquil sleep, is the baby which kept her company on the journey into the unknown.

But the mute marble in Ashbourne Church breaks its silence to tell the story of a tragic sequel for, instead of binding the parents together in the grief they shared, it is said to have resulted in mutual separation and the complete breakdown of their marital relationship. It happened when Penelope's sixth birthday was drawing near; at which time she fell desperately and dangerously ill. The physician was summoned, but his resources and medical skill were unable to bring back warmth and colour to the blanched cheeks, nor could he re-kindle the light of recognition in the glazing eyes. Voices were hushed and footsteps muffled in Ashbourne Hall. But the burden proved too heavy and the struggle too great for the little patient, and the frail flicker of life was extinguished. Her books and toys were sadly put away.

Tradition says that the parents had disagreed as to the choice of a doctor and when the illness proved fatal their feelings towards each other were so bitter that they parted at the graveside to meet no more. Which gives pathetic point and significance to the epitaph:

TO PENELOPE
Only child of Sir Brooke Boothby and Dame Susannah Boothby,

Born April 11th, 1785; Died March 13th, 1791.
She was in form and intellect most exquisite.

The unfortunate parents ventured their all on this frail bark,
and the wreck was total.

Around the tombstone are inscriptions in the four languages with which the precocious Penelope is said to have been familiar.

Penelope lived with her parents at Ashbourne Hall. She was born there forty years after the mansion had been occupied by Bonnie Prince Charlie and his officers. The name of Charles and members of his military staff had been chalked on the doors of the various rooms in which they had been billeted, and the letters had been traced over with white paint to make them more permanent mementoes of the occasion. The Boothbys also had a London house and were acquainted with the artist, Sir Joshua Reynolds, whose studio was often visited by Penelope. At the age of sixty-six, when his sight was beginning to fail, Sir Joshua was commissioned to paint a portrait of the three years' old Penelope, and subsequently she was transfixed by paint and canvas for the enjoyment of future generations. The little girl was portrayed wearing an old-fashioned mob-cap which had belonged to the artist's grandmother. It is a winsome portrait, as she sits so demurely with her mittened hands folded upon her lap, and wearing a white dress with a broad sash around the waist. The portrait was painted in July, 1788.

A charming little story is told of the friendship which existed between Penelope and the painter whose portrait brought her a fame she never lived to enjoy. It concerns an occasion when Penelope's nurse was ill in bed and it was discovered that her little charge was missing. The alarm was immediately raised and a frantic search made of both house and grounds. Eventually it occurred to the nurse that she may have strayed away to Sir Joshua's studio to which messengers were despatched and found her quite innocently playing with a palette knife as she chatted to the artist busy at his easel.

For more than a century the portrait of Penelope gazed pensively from the walls of Ashbourne Hall, beguiling the affections of its occupants and claiming the admiration of its visitors. It was a fortune in a frame. It was worth its weight in gold. Coveted by connoisseurs of art, it then became the property of the Earl of Dudley who purchased it for eleven hundred guineas at the Windus sale in 1859, and later, after being on display in 1885 at Burlington House, it was acquired by Mr. Daniel Thwaites for £20,000. And artist and sitter had been dead for nearly a hundred years.

But the personality of little Penelope was to live on: not merely in moulded marble created by Thomas Banks but in the warmth and colour which Reynolds had imparted to his canvas. Marble is a medium which gives realism to death; but canvas retains the spirit and essence of life. One makes a shroud for mortality; the other weaves a robe of immortality. Long after her death, the spirit of Penelope continued to haunt the spheres of art, invading the fields of poetry, sculpture and literature. In his *Sorrows Sacred to Penelope,* her father wrote:-

Well has thy classic chisel, Banks, expressed,
The graceful lineaments of that fine form
Which late with conscious beauty warm,
Now here beneath does in dread silence rest.

That form, as fair as fancy ever drew,
The marble cold inanimate retains,
But of the radiant smile that round her threw
Joys that beguiled my soul of mortal pains,
And each divine expression's varying hue
A little senseless clay alone remains.

During the year 1879, Miss Edie Talmage caused a revival of interest in the portrait when she decided to impersonate the child, painted nearly a century before, at a fancy dress ball in London, and the sequel was that Sir John Everett Millais decided to make her the subject of his famous picture, 'Cherry Ripe.' Incidentally, while speaking of portraits, it may be of some interest to know that Penelope's father, Sir Brooke Boothby, was painted in a reclining posture by Joseph Wright, of Derby, and this portrait is included in the Tate collection.

For many years Ashboune has been a shrine of pilgrimage to art lovers anxious to see the marble figure of Penelope with its touching story. A certain Mrs. William Robinson, widow of a clergyman, commissioned Sir Francis Chantrey to carve a monument to the memory of her two daughters who had died in girlhood at Lichfield, and she recommended he sculptor to make a study of the Ashbourne monument before engaging upon the work.

Ebenezer Rhodes, in his *Derbyshire Tourist's Guide*, tells how he was present on the occasion of Chantrey's visit to Ashbourne and was present when the design was actually conceived and carried into effect. He is at considerable pains to defend his friend from the contemporary insinuations that an assistant was originally responsible for the design, quoting an article in the *Eclectic Review* of 1828 in which the writer refers to the established practice of assistants carrying out the preliminary work of dressing and preparing stone ready for their master's finishing touch. 'Here is obviously no necessity for the intervention of the master, excepting in the design and model; nor is it, as we have understood, by any means unusual for the first of these to be furnished by artists of readier invention than some sculptors are supposed to possess. We have heard, in particular, that one of our ablest men, and another of very inferior eminence, have been *altogether* indebted, the one to Smirke, and the other to Stothard, for their original sketches.'

Chantrey and Rhodes enjoyed a similar relationship to that of Johnson and Boswell, and while the sculptor appeared indifferent to the allegations, his friend stoutly defended him against such inuendo. Without the sculptor's knowledge or consent, he gaved personal testimony to what happened after they had travelled from Bakewell to Ashbourne. Arriving late, they deferred their visit to the church until the following morning when the sculptor made an outline drawing of the Boothby monument. After spending the rest of the day in Dovedale, and while waiting for the London coach, Rhodes reports that, 'About ten o'clock, Chantrey took out his Sketch-book. A few specimens of ferns, brought from Dovedale, occupied his attention for the first half-hour; he then told me not to disturb him, but to amuse myself in my own way, as he intended to make a drawing for the Lichfield monument before the coach arrived. This was done, and the design he at this time made, with scarcely any variation whatever, was subsequently executed in marble, and shortly afterwards submitted to public inspection in the model-room of the Royal Academy, at Somerset House. The sensation which this exquisie production created has had no parallel in the annals of modern art. Three of Canova's fine works were in the same exhibition: his beautiful figure of Hebe, now in the possession of the Duke of Devonshire, at Chatsworth; his Terpsichore, and a bust of Peace: yet, notwithstanding the acknowledged excellence of these masterly productions, and the novelty of their exhibition in London, the group of the two children robbed the great Italian sculptor of his laurels. His statues were seen, and, of course, highly admired; but Chantrey's "children" excited a far more intense degree of interest. The crowd that hung over them in silent abstraction was, for many successive days, so dense, that the monument was approached with difficulty, and by many but imperfectly seen. The sculptor, after the close of the exhibition, wished to have a painting of this group; and, from a desire to serve Stothard, he gave him the commission for the picture.'

Ashbourne began to lose some of its glamour to nearby Lichfield. The sentimental pilgrims who had congregated round Penelope's tomb were now flocking to Lichfield in increasing numbers. Reynold's little friend had found rivals for popularity in the relatively unknown Robinson children who nestled together in the quiet aisle of the great cathedral, the younger one clutching her little posy of snowdrops. Visitors to Ashbourne began to inspect the tomb of Penelope with prejudiced eyes, comparing it with the work of Chantrey, and quite often to its disadvantage. An elderly female verger, when conducting a party round the church in 1829, overheard two of the number discussing the rival merits of the two monuments and, upon reaching agreement that the work of Chantrey was superior to that of Banks, the old lady remarked with asperity: 'Humph! the like of that's what I now hear every day. Hang that fellow Chanty or Canty, or what you call him! I wish he had never been born.'

I suppose we can understand the lopsided loyalty which provoked the statement. Perhaps we, in the same circumstances, might have expressed the same opinion. But the old lady had no need to fear, for Penelope had found her niche in art and history and will continue to reign in sovereign state in the hearts of those who know her sad and simple story.

Joseph Wright

The Derby Artist

'CERTAINLY no man has painted Derbyshire scenery like him; his pictures of the High Tor, at Matlock, are a revelation - marvellous reflections on canvas of the limestone rocks, strangely riven, and foliage-clad, that rise high above the rushing waters of the Derwent; and there is a great fascination in his best known work, "The Orrery", with its wondrous light and shadows playing on the faces and forms of those who are listening so intently to the philosopher's lecture.'

This is one of the many tributes paid to the art of Joseph Wright, familiarly known as 'Wright of Derby'. Although he is not esteemed by art critics as achieving the same status as Gainsborough, Reynolds, Romney and Wilson; yet in the admiring eyes of a layman like the writer -- who admittedly lacks professional qualification and whose judgement is no doubt weighted by prejudice -- he ranks as the greatest artist Derbyshire has produced.

Born at Derby in 1734, Joseph Wright was the son of prosperous and middle-class parents who were indulgent enough to encourage his aptitude for art. A contemporary of Sir Joshua Reynolds, he was fortunate to study under the same master, Thomas Hudson, spending two years in London and later returning for further tuition. He began his career as a portrait painter and his sitters included such Derbyshire personalities as Sir Richard Arkwright, Dr. Erasmus Darwin, John Whitehurst, Sir Brooke Boothby, Samuel Crompton, Canon Thomas Seward and many others. Some were members of obscure families whose very names are forgotten, but whose portraits have survived.

It was to discharge one such commission that Wright paid a visit to my own village of Eyam, and I am rather disappointed that -- unlike Sir Francis Chantrey at a later date -- he was not inspired to make a sketch of the picturesque cottages where bubonic plague had broken out a century before. For it was to 'Delf View', a small mansion situated right opposite the cottage where the plague was delivered in a bale of cloth, that the eminent artist came with brushes, easel, palette and paints to portray Sarah Carver and her little daughter. Like many of his other sitters, Sarah made no particular impact on contemporary society and is only remembered for the fact that Wright transferred her charm and grace to canvas. The pulpit of Eyam Church had been occupied between 1680 and 1683 by a Rev.

Charles Carver, but I have not been able to establish any family link. The young lady is wearing a wrist ornament which contains a miniature of perhaps her husband or father, and this is one of the distinctive touches of the artist, although it may be easily missed by only casual examination. 'Delf View' was the property of Marmaduke Middleton who may have been one of Sarah's descendants, and the painting later hung in Leam Hall until it was donated by Mrs. G. Rose-Innes to augment the Wright Collection at Derby Art Gallery.

For a number of years Wright worked outside the county, spending three years at Liverpool where he painted many local industrialists and manufacturers by whom such portraits were regarded as symbols of social status. He was less successful when settled at fashionable Bath in 1775, expecting to inherit the popularity of Gainsborough who had moved to London. He had a sensitive and rather nervous temperament, and was easily irritated and depressed. So, disappointed by lack of response from the population of this sophisticated city of which he had entertained such high hopes, he returned in 1777 to his native Derby.

In addition to his work in portraiture, Wright became enchanted with the portrayal of dramatic scenes in which light seems to struggle for mastery over darkness with the most spectacular results. Sometimes the light was created by man: the reflections from a forge, a lighthouse beam, a frenzy of fireworks, or children blowing fragile bubbles by candlelight. Sometimes the light was natural: the pale silver of moonlight, the spectrum of a rainbow, or a volcano weeping tears of fire. One picture gives the impression of a wild choreography of colour; another is imbued with a sense of serenity and peace.

The artist lived during an exciting and adventurous period. He was much influenced by the advances being made in science, chemistry, commerce and industry, and his experiments in the new genre was to make his work remembered when otherwise it may have been forgotten. His works depicting artificial light contain an alchemy of magic and mystery, as illustrated by such paintings as The Orrery, Experiment with an Air Pump, Academy by Lamplight, The Alchymist, Girl Reading a Letter, and many more. Referring to his use of this technique, Benedict Nicholson wrote of the influence exerted on Wright by certain painters in the Netherlands who practised in a similar media. 'In Honthurst he found the artist who suited his temperament best. From him he learnt that the way to convey wonder was to group men around a table, and let them all concentrate on one inanimate object, and sometimes to make the light behind a curtain or somebody's sleeve so that it should not get diffused but be reflected with the same intensity on their features, thus heightening the sense of drama; the only difference being that whereas Honthurst (or other artists affected by the same passions such as Stomer or Terbrugghen by whom Wright was also influenced without realising it) would take the bread that Christ was breaking as the object of the audience's attention, Wright would take the source of wonder in his own day.'

After becoming so fascinated with the appeal of light and shadow in both human activity and natural phenomenon, and having developed his techniques to perfection, Wright's paintings were much in demand from wealthy industrialists and aristocratic families. He was at the height of popularity and, shortly after his marriage, he and his wife toured Italy and visited Naples between November, 1773, and August, 1775. During this period their first child was born and christened Romana.

Wright first exhibited at the Royal Academy in 1778 and was elected A.R.A. three years later. Owing to a disagreement he declined full membership when it was offered in 1784 and submitted no works between the years 1782 and 1788. After resuming residence at Derby in 1777, he continued painting portraits but seemed to lose his obsession for 'candlelight' studies, and turned his attention to landscapes. He seldom left home, except to visit London for exhibitions of his work, and on two occasions spent summer visits in the Lake District. Both his Derbyshire and Lake District scenes found ready purchasers.

Wright died in 1797 at the age of sixty-three, and his works are treasured in homes and art galleries both in this country and abroad. A considerable number have been collected and centralised -- as is most fitting--at Derby Art Gallery where, one feels, the artist would have been proud and gratified that his native place should so recognise and value his work and worth.

Grace Murray

'The Broken Heart'

'GRACE Murray, you have broken my heart!'

Grace Murrey, is virtually a forgotten figure in history, but the person whom she provoked to utter this anguished comment is remembered throughout the civilised world. His name has long been a household word and his portraits and monumental statues rival in number some of the most distinguished royal and political personages in history. Innumerable books have been written about his life and activities and he has been the subject of radio, television and film script writers. Such was his popularity that enterprising potters made him the subject of equestrian models, figurines, busts and even toby-jug ware. The words of this silver tongued orator have been translated into many languages and his literary works have the same imperishable quality as those of Shakespeare and Bunyan. His name -- John Wesley.

Yet Grace Murray, this almost unknown figure, innocent of guile and without the exercise of conscious subtlety and charm, captured the heart that was so 'strangely warmed' in a London meeting that Wesley's subsequent ministry brought the English nation to its knees in penitence and prayer. The words and music of hymns he and his brother composed put a 'new song' into the mouth of our nation when it had nearly lost its hope and faith, and became responsible for one of the greatest reformatory movements in the Christian religion.

The name of Grace Murray, or Bennet as she became after her marriage, is probably forgotten in Chinley where she lived for many years and where she and her husband lie buried in the former Independent Chapel; a place of worship which has associations with that great Derbyshire revivalist of earlier days, the Rev. William Bagshawe, Apostle of the Peak. The name and reputation of Grace would have been assured of greater permanence had she accepted Wesley's proposal of marriage, for it is obvious that she would have figured more prominently in the records of religious romance than did the wife of his later choice. Many women would have been proud, flattered and honoured to have received the advances of so distinguished a personality and few would have declined him and incurred the sad reproach -- 'You have broken my heart.'

Grace Murray was a nurse in charge of the Newcastle Orphan House established by Wesley and, having fallen victim to her charms, he made his offer of marriage. But Grace was not a person to be swept off her feet by such an attractive offer, and also there was another John contending for the favour of her hand. This John had fallen in love with Grace when a hospital patient under her care. His name was John Bennet. John was a student of law and theology and had been greatly influenced by the preaching of David Taylor, a member of the Countess of Huntingdon's evangelical movement. He had been so impressed by the preaching of Taylor that he invited him to conduct services at his father's house at Chinley. Taylor preached at Chapel Milton in 1741 and it was there that the first Methodist society was established in the Peak District.

The new movement spread rapidly and Bennet undertook the work of administration, paying regular visits on horseback to encourage the new 'causes'. Wesley paid several visits to Chinley and preached in surrounding villages. Bennet rode with him in 1744 to London to attend the first Methodist Conference and was appointed to take the minutes of the various meetings. He also inaugurated the system of quarterly meetings which still provides the administrative machinery for Methodist circuits.

On the 31st August, 1748, a party of four travellers rode into Chinley. One was Grace Murray, another John Wesley, the third John Bennet and a fourth person named Mackford. After a brief call at the home of Bennet's father, Wesley continued his journey to London and Mackford proceeded north. Grace stayed for a week and it is obvious that Bennet took full advantage of the occasion to improve his relationship with the fair visitor. But, as in the case with Wesley, Grace did not make an impulsive decision and her impatient suitor was obliged to wait. At the end of the week, while returning to Leeds from Chinley, John used all the arts of eloquence and persuasion to secure Grace's favour, wresting from her a partial promise of acceptance. The next year she capitulated and they were married at Newcastle.

Well might the disappointed Wesley cry: 'Grace Murray, you have broken my heart!'

Within a couple of years, Bennet seceded from Methodism and established an Independent Chapel near Warrington. He also seems to have severed his friendship with the founder, for Wesley never visited Chinley again. Ten years after his marriage, at the age of 45, Bennet died, leaving his widow with a family of five boys. She returned to Chapel Milton and lived a widow for forty-five years, dying at the age of nearly ninety.

Molly Bray

The Ashford Dwarf

HAD Molly (or correctly Mary) Bray lived a couple of centuries earlier, she might well have been arraigned on a charge of witchcraft. Known to history as the Ashford Dwarf, she was only three feet tall, or perhaps one should say three feet small; yet she terrorised her neighbours by spiteful threats and frequent outbursts of temper. Not only was she an object of fear to the children of Ashford-in-the-Water, but many of their parents took great pains to avoid provoking her wrath and malice, and often proved easy victims to her aptitude for intimidation. It may be that she was embittered by her physical defects and disabilities, and envious of the endowments of women upon whom Nature had looked with greater favour. Or maybe she rejoiced in a sinister sense of power with which to inspire dread in those about her.

A portrait of Molly's diminutive figure was published by White

Watson, the Bakewell geologist, but copies of this are now very rare. One used to hang in the Devonshire Arms at Ashford-in-the-Water, only a stone's throw from the site of her former home.

This eccentric person lived in a thatched cottage opposite the village church, but this has long since been demolished. During its occupation by Molly it was described as a filthy hovel and had few attractions for the neighbouring gossips. She herself was described as usually 'wearing a kind of wide-awake hat, an old scarlet cloak or bedgown, a thin handkerchief around her head and chin, and a breasted pinafore which was extremely ragged at the nether extremities. She always walked with an over-hand knob-stick, and had a peculiar habit of squatting down on the roads with her legs tucked under tailor-wise.' She adopted this posture when carriages passed between Bakewell and Buxton and her pitiful appearance and appeals for charity usually resulted in some gifts of money.

Like many elderly women of her day, Molly enjoyed the luxury of a pipe of tobacco, and one can imagine her sitting beside her door with wisps of smoke curling from the stained bowl of her clay pipe. She was said to be slovenly in her dress, dirty in appearance and altogether careless about personal hygiene. Yet these facts did not appear to curtail her length of life by causing any serious illness or disease. She was secretly accused of being a witch and guilty of participation in the black arts, but no positive allegations were made to this effect for the simple reason that few would care to invoke her displeasure. Nor was she averse to using this ill reputation to advance her own interests by the exercise of blackmail, intimidation and other pressures.

On one occasion Molly discovered and threatened to expose a flirtation between a certain resident of the village named Soldier John and Widow Alice Thorpe, insisting upon making them respectable citizens and members of society by marrying them over a broomstick. Before she died, Molly gave the village undertaker strict instructions about the making of her coffin, threatening that she would return and haunt him if these were not carried out to the very last letter. Needless to say, her funeral was conducted with all due reverence and circumspection. She lived to be nearly ninety years of age and her obituary in the parish register of Ashford-in-the-Water stated: 'Buried March 11, 1811, Mary Bray.'

Kitty Hudson

'The Human Pincushion'

WE might imagine that such a title as this belonged to some performer in a circus or travelling show; to some human porcupine bristling with spikes or spines, or at least to some feminine fakir with a facility for reclining upon a bed of nails. But Kitty Hudson was none of these. She was never billed as a circus attraction or stage performer engaged in some act designed to tempt the coins of those curious and credulous people who are easily deceived by sleight of hand and overawed by deeds of daring and skill.

Kitty Hudson was not a native of Derbyshire, but ended her days in the county. Born at Arnold, Notts., in 1765, she went at the age of six to live with her grandfather, Mr. White, who was sexton of St. Mary's Church, Nottingham. A servant used to enlist Kitty's aid when sweeping the aisles and dusting the pews, and rewarded the girl with a stick of toffee for every mouthful of pins she picked up while carrying out this work. This unhealthy habit became so strong in Kitty that she could not eat, drink, or sleep without having pins or needles in her mouth, and she often had to leave her bed to obtain a supply during periods of insomnia.

She was admitted to the General Hospital, Nottingham, on June 12th, 1785, and underwent an astonishing series of operations during which a great number of pins, needles and pieces of carious bone were extracted from her feet, legs, arms and other parts of the body. At this time both her breasts were removed. Surgery, in those days, was both crude and cruel, and anaesthetics were a thing of the future. Sir James Young Simpson, discoverer of the medical uses of chloroform, was not born until 1811 and Kitty must have suffered excruciating pain as the result of her hospital treatment. However, she was greatly cheered and comforted by a fellow patient, John Goddard, who suffered from a complaint that caused him the loss of an eye. The two had been childhood sweethearts and John used to promise her that, if she lost all her limbs, so long as life itself was spared, he would become her husband. And this was the inspiration to which Kitty attributed her powers of endurance.

Six months after being discharged from hospital, their dream came true. John married Kitty and eventually they had a family of nineteen children, none of whom lived to the age of eighteen.

After being bereaved of her husband, Kitty later became the wife of Henry Ludlam, of Pinxton, where she spent the rest of her days.

She was described as being 'nearly six feet tall and pins and needles continued to come to the surface of her body until the day of her death. A black spot appeared on the skin and soon began to fester, then the head of the pin showed and after this had been drawn out the place healed over ...'

William Newton

'The Minstrel of the Peak'

THERE is nothing very picturesque or romantic about the appearance of the Cockey Farm. It is just a typical Peakland farmhouse; plain but sturdy, sheltered beneath trees and guarded by buildings, outhouses and perhaps a few hayricks. Lying midway between Bretton Clough and the hamlet of Abney, this lonely farm is situated among fields which give the impression that they are still closely related to the moors from which they have been wrested by the husbandry of many generations. And, as a complete contrast, gliders from nearby Camp Hill skim silently along like wooden pterodactyls from some prehistoric Noah's Ark.

Yet there is an element of romance and historical interest about Cockey Farm which is never suspected by many ramblers who pass through its yard when following the footpath from Bretton Clough to Abney. For it was here that William Newton, the 'Minstrel of the Peak', was born on November 25th, 1750. Newton was not a poet of outstanding genius, nor did his gift for weaving words into rhyme bring him financial reward or any enduring measure of renown. Yet he is remembered among such local laureates of literature as Richard Furness and Peter Cunningham, both of Eyam, John Howe, of Ashford-in-the-Water, John Gisborne, of Darley Dale, whose poems were praised by Wordsworth, and the Howitts -- William, Mary and Richard.

The earliest record concerning the poet is in Hope Parish Register which contains the entry: 'December 25th., 1750, baptised William, son of George and Mary Newton'. That Christmas Day christening was marked in later years by the composition of Christmas carols, some of which were set to music by Tideswell's famous bass singer, Samuel Slack.

Little is known of Newton's childhood except that his father's financial circumstances were such as to restrict William's education to the limited curriculum of a dame school and the services of a writing master. However, he appears to have made the most of opportunities afforded and his desire for learning was further stimulated by the perusal of books he occasionally picked up in houses where he was working as a carpenter. This was the trade of his father, but William was not content to spend his time repairing farm wagons, making and mending field gates or household furniture, and, tempted by better wages and working conditions, he left the farmhouse where he was born and obtained work at the thriving cotton mills at Cressbrook. After being employed as a carpenter-mechanic he obtained the position of head carpenter for the Duke of Devonshire who was then engaged in building the famous Crescent at Buxton. He later returned to a Cressbrook mill where he earned a salary of £50 per year making and maintaining mill machinery.

Newton was now happily married to Helen Cook, a young woman three years his junior, but their tranquil life was shattered by sudden tragedy. Fire broke out at the mill where he worked and this building --along with the cottage he occupied -- was burned to the ground. This was in 1788 and the couple were both homeless and penniless, for they had lost everything they possessed and were considered fortunate in having escaped alive. His tools, valued at £30, were all destroyed.

Miss Anna Seward, who had befriended Newton some years before, came to his rescue by canvassing subscriptions from a few influential friends to relieve the immediate distress of the couple, and followed up this generous gesture by obtaining Newton the chance of a third partnership in a cotton mill at Monsal Dale. He was required, however, to invest £200 capital in the firm, and this amount was scraped together largely by the help of his godmother who had shared his home before the fire. By the sale of some property, which was her 'sole support', she raised £150 and the balance of £50 was advanced by Miss Seward. Thus the poet was given the opportunity to retrieve his misfortune and five years later he was worth £1,000.

Miss Seward's patronage of Newton dated from about 1780 when her father's curate, the Rev. Peter Cunningham, of Eyam, brought to her notice some of his poems. She had taken a benevolent, if somewhat condescending, interest in the young poet and conferred upon him the flattering title -- 'Minstrel of the Peak.' It was largely due to her influence that his poems were commended to the public by the *Gengleman's Magazine* and other contemporary journals, including the *Sheffield Iris.*

As the 'Swan of Lichfield' Miss Seward commanded wide respect in her day, and the books she wrote were a source of considerable revenue to publishers. But, although her volumes of poetry and correspondence ran into many editions during and shortly after her lifetime, the judgment of posterity has been such that any modern publisher would hesitate to resurrect them from their musty tomb in the graveyard of literature. Her reputation as a writer brought the Swan into contact with many notable personalities including Dr. Johnson, Dr. Darwin, Hayley, Squire Mundy and Sir Walter Scott whom she appointed as her literary executor. After her death, when he was preparing material for publication, Scott confided in a letter to Johanna Baillie that 'her posthumous poetry was absolutely execrable.' Miss Mary R.Mitford wrote acidly: 'I wonder by what accident Miss Seward came by her fame. Setting aside her pedantry and presumption, there is no poet male or female who ever clothed so few ideas in so many words. She is all tinkling and tinsel -- a sort of Dr. Darwin in petticoats.' Her portrait was painted by George Romney and Tilly Kettle.

Miss Seward appears to have made no attempt to disguise the sense of social superiority with which she regarded Newton and referred to him with an irritating air of patronage which, one might imagine, would have filled the sensitive soul of a poet with deep humiliation. But no, Newton seems to have been quite undismayed by her imperiousness, and gratefully accepted her condescension as no more than his due reward. Unlike Richard Furness or Ebenezer Elliott, the Corn Law Rhymer, Newton restrained his poetical philosophy from developing into a campaign (with one exception) against social iniquities or political taxation, and confined his muse to the then popular styles of poetry which were liberal in the use of classical embellishment.

The one exception was a vigorous protest against the existing penal system which condoned the practice of sometimes gibbeting the bodies of criminals who had suffered execution. Newton's poem was largely inspired by the sentence passed upon Anthony Lingard, a 21 years' old man who had been hung for the murder of Hannah Oliver, a toll-keeper at Wardlow Miers. Lingard's body was hung in chains near the scene of the crime, and hundreds of people flocked to see the morbid spectacle. So great were the crowds of sightseers that pedlars and hucksters erected booths for the sale of their merchandise.

John Longden, a Methodist preacher who kept the Snake Inn, preached a memorable sermon at the foot of the gibbet. He had walked 14 miles to take services at Tideswell, but found the chapel deserted on his arrival. Learning that his congregation had played truant in order to see the gibbet, Longden joined in the pilgrimage to Wardlow and, taking his stand beneath the gibbet, he delivered a stirring exhortation to penitence. Longden's sermon caused a sensation, but its influence was not so widely felt as was the sermon Newton preached in his poem. The theme of the poem was an imagined scene when, during a storm, Lingard's father paid a nocturnal visit to the site of the gibbet. As a result of its publication, steps were taken to abolish the inhuman practice of displaying the bodies of criminals to public curiosity, and because of the ensuing agitation, the Wardlow Gibbet is said to have been the last seen in England.

Incidentally, a side effect of the incident is said to have been responsible for the opening to public traffic of the road through Chatsworth Park. Soldiers accompanying Lingard's body from the place of execution at Derby to the site of the crime at Wardlow, lost their way at Rowsley. Instead of proceeding by Bakewell, they continued through Beeley and Chatsworth Park to Baslow and so to Wardlow. An ancient law specified that if a corpse was carried over a private road it became a public right of way, and pins were formerly paid or nails driven into gate-posts for the privilege of using the road. But the soldiers paid no such peppercorn and freedom of passage was afterwards claimed.

Although critics may accuse Newton of affectation in his poetry, they cannot make the same charge against his personality, for he was a modest and unassuming man, thereby earning the respect of several distinguished people. Both Mary Sterndale, whose *Vignettes of Derbyshire* was published in 1824, and Sir Francis Chantrey, the sculptor, paid tribute to the generous treatment received by the pauper children who lived and worked in his mill.

The children under Newton's care were well clothed and fed; slept in well ventilated dormitories; were allowed ample time for recreation, which included cultivating their own patches of garden, while boys with an aptitude for music were provided with facilities for developing this talent. Relatives and friends were given the opportunity to visit the children at regular intervals, and inspectors had complete freedom to carry out their duties. On Sundays the children walked to Tideswell Church, but if the weather was wet or in winter, Sunday School classes were held on the mill premises. This was greatly in contrast to the harsh treatment received by children at nearby Litton Mill where they were poorly fed and clothed and worked for twelve or fourteen hours a day.

On one ocasion Miss Seward invited Newton to Buxton where she was staying at one of the fashionable hotels. The invitation was made with some misgivings, as we gather from the text of a letter written to an acquaintance: 'That being of true integrity, that prodigy of self-taught genius, Newton, the minstrel of my native mountains, walks over from Tideswell, his humble home, to pass the day with me to-morrow. To preclude wonder and comments upon my attentions to such an apparent rustic at the public table, I have shown two charming little poems of his, which are deservedly admired here.' A further description from her pen ran: 'Mr. Newton is not ill-looking, but has nothing in his appearance beyond the decent and the clean...To have found, in the compositions of a laborious villager, some bright sparks of genius amid the dross of prosaic vulgarity had been pleasing, though perhaps not wonderful; but the elegance and harmony of Newton's writings, both in prose and verse, are miraculous, when it is remembered that, till Mr. Cunningham distinguished him, he has associated only with the unlettered vulgar.'

These sentiments may be compared with Newton's fulsome expressions of gratitude, as for example:- 'All that your pensive, your lonely friend can return for this unmerited kindness (the gift of one of her books), are the warm effusions of a grateful heart. My walk along the vale of life has not been through a wilderness of sweets. You have scattered in my paths flowers of so agreeable an odour, culled from the bowers of the muses, that will lighten, in many an irksome hour, the weight of manual labour.

William Hayley, the Poet Laureate, upon being asked his opinion of Robert Burns, replied to Miss Seward that 'he admired the Scotch peasant, but do not think him superior to your poetical carpenter.' The passing years -- which always test the true worth of poetry -- have proved the error of Hayley's judgment.

Newton came by chance into contact with the famous Derbyshire sculptor, Sir Francis Chantrey, who noted the incident as follows: 'During a ramble in my own beautiful county (which has scenery I never saw surpassed in any), and descending into Monsal Dale, I overtook a peasant, as I believed, for he wore the ordinary dress of one, and that was tufted with locks of cotton wool adhering to it. I asked some question respecting the road and its neighbourhood, and was cheerfully and civilly answered. Our way lay in the same direction, and we continued our talk; very soon I found myself in glowing contact with a mind awakened to all the touching beauties of the scenery, to poetic expression, and to such an appreciation of the fine arts as astonished and delighted me. The Dale was, or seemed to be, very short; as its termination we approached a cluster of buildings for the manufacture of cotton, a small house, which seemed to grow out of the rock, standing a little apart; into it I was cordially invited, and there I learnt my companion was Mr. Newton, the manager of the concern, also the director, master, and friend of 300 children, which the then existing law of our land permitted to be selected from the orphan asylums and charity hospitals of our large towns. Here I stayed for the remainder of the day, interested, surprised, and charmed in various ways. I took a sketch of my host, and left it with his family -- a slight but expressive token of my gratified feelings.

What a privilege and honour! To enjoy intelligent conversation on a common level without the need for servility as the price of patronage. And, as a bonus, to have one's portrait sketched by an artist of nation-wide reputation!

Newton's retirement was spent at Tideswell where he lived in a house which has since been converted into the Peacock Inn. There he lived in peace and contentment, respected by those with whom he lived and by those whom he had employed. And it was in this township, five miles from the place of his birth and three from the mill beside the winding River Wye where he had made his modest fortune, the Minstrel of the Peak laid down the burden of life at the age of 80 years, and was buried near the sundial within the shadow of the Cathedral of the Peak. Eight days later, on November 11th, 1830, the grave was re-opened to receive the remains of the one who had shared his triumphs and disappointments, his joys and sorrows, his failures and success. Death could not divide the two lives which had grown so closely knit that they almost lived and breathed as one.

Elizabeth Evans

The Dinah Morris of 'Adam Bede'

NOT MANY women in history could claim to have ridden to the gallows with an unmarried mother sentenced to death for the murder of her child. They may have had the compassion but not the courage to identify themselves with a member of their sex condemned to suffer public execution for such a crime. But this was the experience of Elizabeth Evans, a once prominent preacher at Wirksworth who was the prototype of Dinah Morris in the novel *Adam Bede*, and the incident was re-lived in the pages of the story written by her niece, Mary Ann Evans, better known by her pen-name, George Eliot. She also spent the night previous to the execution in the condemned cell with this poor young woman to comfort and strengthen her in facing the forthcoming ordeal.

Many contemporary members of the Church endorsed Paul's insistence to 'let your women keep silence in the church', but some theologians regard this as censure against female gossip and tattling, and not a rebuke directed at women called to the ministry of preaching. In the Acts we find reference to a certain evangelist, Philip of Caesarea, who 'had four daughters, virgins, which did prophesy.' In other words they were preachers whose oratory was acceptable to the early Church. But opposition to women preachers was strong in the days of Elizabeth Evans and this feminine firebrand at one time seceded from the Wesleyans to join the Arminian Methodists, but later resumed membership with her former persuasion.

In the epilogue of *Adam Bede*, the hero says of Dinah, 'Conference has forbid the women preaching, and she's given it up, all but talking to the people a bit in their houses.' Seth says, 'and a sore pity it was o'

Conference; and if Dinah had seen as I did, we'd ha' left the Wesleyans and joined a body that ud put no bonds on Christian liberty.' But Dinah tactfully changed the subject.

Elizabeth's husband, Samuel, was a preacher and held services in the Tape Mill where he was manager. Samuel is believed to have supplied the character of Seth Bede in the novel, although he appears to have had the physique of Adam, often walking from Derby Market Place to Wirksworth in two hours -- a distance of thirteen miles. Visitors have travelled long distances to see the Tape Mill and the once thatched cottage across the way 'standing sideways to the road with a little bit of potato-ground before it.' In addition to the thatch having been substituted with slate, the interior has undergone some structural alteration since the days when it was occupied by the Evans.

Elizabeth Evans had no ambitions to be famous. Indeed, she was so modest and unassuming that she expressed the wish that her grave in Wirksworth churchyard should not be marked by any headstone, but the contemporary verger -- old Gill Pickard -- felling that some form of memorial should identify the spot without violating her request, obtained permission to plant a copper beech to distinguish the site and many pilgrims have sought out this simple shrine. Her husband was buried in grave No. 1400 in the public cemetery, having died at No. 4 The Causeway, Wirksworth.

Mrs. Evans (nee Tomlinson) was born at Newbold in Leicestershire, removing in girlhood to Nottingham where she worked as a 'lace-mender'. She was converted to Methodism in 1797 at a small chapel at Beck Barn and became an earnest and enthusiastic evangelist, adopting simple Quaker-like dress and achieving considerable success in the preaching profession. Much of her ministry was carried out in the open air.

During the period she lived in Nottingham, a young woman named Mary Voce was sentenced to death for poisoning her youngest child, and Elizabeth and a friend obtained permission to visit the condemned mother in prison. They remained with her day and night until the morning of the execution and eventually, as a result of their sympathy, prayers and entreaties, Mary was brought to the point of penitence for her crime. On the day of execution, Nottingham was the scene of a great public demonstration. Escorted by huge crowds and a procession of Methodists singing hymns, the two young women rode with Mary on her final journey in the hangman's cart to Gallows Hill. This incident provided inspiration for the moving story of Hetty Sorrel which is so vividly related in the novel and which is brought to a conclusion in the shortest chapter of the book—'The Last Moment'. This chapter consists of but a single page and begins: 'It was a sight that some people remembered better even than their own sorrows—the sight in that gray clear morning when the fatal cart with the two young women in it was descried by the waiting, watching multitude, cleaving its way towards the hideous symbol of deliberately-inflicted death.' The novelist had greater compassion than the Nottingham jury for, although feeling she could not acquit the guilty mother, she granted her a last minute reprieve and commuted the death sentence to that of transportation for life.

Hetty's story is the agony column of the novel; a triumph of journalism. It inspired the literary stratagem which provides more than just an incidental theme of the novel, for the human appeal of the story would be much diminished and would not have attracted so large a readership response, if it had only been based on the merits of a woman preacher. Such a plot in itself would not have had sufficient uniqueness to claim the reader's interest, but integrated with a story like that of Hetty Sorrel it could scarcely fail to captivate the imagination by its rarity and reality.

Elizabeth worked for a period at Tutbury, meeting her future husband in Ashbourne during the year 1802. They were married at St. Mary's Church, Nottingham, and after living in that town and at Norbury and Derby, settled at Wirksworth. They were first affiliated in membership with the Wesleyan Ebenezer Chapel, but later became members of the Chapel at Folly Corner, Warmbrook. Some time after the death of Mrs. Evans, this congregation transferred to the one in St. John Street now named in her honour, the Bede Memorial Chapel. A tablet bears the inscription: *To the memory of Elizabeth Evans, known to the world as Dinah Morris, who during many years proclaimed alike in the open-air, the sanctuary, and from house to house, the love of Christ; also Samuel Evans, a faithful local preacher.*

Other mementoes include the quaint wooden pulpit she occupied when preaching in the old Folly Corner Chapel, and which was removed to the Memorial Chapel. Ebenezer Chapel contains a book-rest made from an old pulpit from which she used to preach, and in the County Library may be seen her Grandfather's clock. Other personal relics in private possession include a contemporary portrait, purse, spectacles, lace mob-cap, crepe shawl, silver brooch, a well-thumbed Bible, a bed-sheet marked 'E.E. 1823, No. 12', and a funeral card printed for the occasion of her interment on May 14th, 1849. She died on May 9th at No. 35 John Street in the 74th year of her age.

George Eliot's father, Robert Evans, was born between Norbury and Ashbourne in a two storeyed brick cottage on the roadside with a strip of garden and the adjoining wheel-wright's shop' where he plied this craft before moving across the River Dove to Ellaston in 'Loamshire.' The novelist had her father in mind when portraying the carefully observed character who played the title role in her story, and who (in the novel) married Dinah Morris, whereas in real life Elizabeth married Samuel Evans who figured as Seth Bede.

The correctness of George Eliot's description of Wirksworth (Snowfield) has often been disputed, but we must remember that she lived in a more hospitable climate, and to her it doubtless 'lay grim, stony and unsheltered up the sides of a steep hill' and was 'a hungry land where lead mines had been and were no longer.' Dovedale is recognised as the Eaglesdale where 'in two or three hours' ride the traveller might exchange a bleak, treeless region intersected by lines of cold grey stone, for one where his road wound under the shelter of up-swelling hills, muffled with hedgerows and long meadow grass and thick corn.' Ellaston is believed to be 'Hayslope' and Middleton-by Wirksworth is 'Sloman's End—a 'little grey desolate-looking hamlet unscreened by sheltering trees.'

A now vanished landmark, victim of the local quarrying industry, was Monkey Bridge which spanned a dizzy gorge and marked the place where, according to local tradition, Adam made his romantic proposal of marriage. 'Looking into her sincere eyes, he vowed: "Then we'll never part any more, Dinah, till death parts us." And they kissed each other with a deep joy.'

Phoebe Brown

The Amazon of Matlock Green

IF Phoebe Brown had been living today, she might have made a modest fortune on the stage by tearing up telephone directories, bending rods of iron, challenging contestants in the wrestling ring, and performing other feats of strength and endurance. With her outstanding 'physical attractions' she would no doubt have been welcomed in cinema and T.V. studios as a useful 'extra ' for comedy productions. She might even have qualified as a Miss Universe and been included in the Guiness Book of Records. But she does not even rank along with such Matlock celebrities as Sir George Newnes, John Smedley and Adam Woolley.

Renowned in her day as 'the Amazon of Matlock Green', Phoebe was quite a tourist attraction and visitors to Matlock regarded her as one of the 'sights' of the town, straining to catch a glimpse of her stalwart figure or seeking the privilege of a personal interview. Phoebe's chief claims to historical recognition rest in her remarkable masculine strength and habits which caused one writer to describe her as being of 'dubious sex.' A somewhat prophetic figure of the women's lib movement, she invaded almost every sphere of male activity. She was reputed to be a dexterous carpenter, mason and smith, and was noted both as a pugilist and duellist, 'fighting with the weapons she produced at the forge as well as with her fists.' It is recorded that she could 'ride or break a horse with the first jockey at Newmarket or the boldest rider in the country; pass her opinion on the value of the animal with as much judgement as a dealer and could shoot at a target with as much skill as a sharpshooter.'

The historian, Hutton, was personally acquainted with Phoebe and left the following account of some of her activities:- 'Her step is more manly than a man's, and can cover 40 miles a day. She undertakes any kind of manual labour, as holding the plough, driving the team, thatching the barn, using the flail; but her chief avocation is breaking horses at a guinea a week. Her voice is more than masculine; with the wind in her favour she can send it a mile. She is fond of Milton, Pope and Shakespeare; she is well taught and performs on several instruments, as the flute, violin, harpsichord, and supports the bass viol in Matlock church.' Phoebe acquired her knowledge of music from a travelling harper, and when a lady presented her with a harpsichord she forthwith set to work and built a wing on her cottage for its accommodation. This was not her only architectural accomplishment for she also superintended the building of a house in Matlock Dale called Cliffe House.

Like many people of her day, Phoebe had great faith in omens, predictions, charms and other similar superstitions. Also, in spite of her physical strength, she had at least one psychological weakness, in that she was haunted by the dread of people conspiring to rob her. In order to prevent this eventuality, her home was transformed into an armoury and arsenal of weapons, many of which she had made. Her walls were adorned with muskets, fowling-pieces, daggers, and cutlasses, and she often added to her collection by forging spears and bayonets from odd pieces of steel. One dark night, when walking along a lonely stretch of road, Phoebe was attacked by a man with the intention of molesting her. But he met more than his match and came off worst for the encounter. When I mentioned this incident at a W.I. meeting at Castleton, one member of the audience made the heartfelt and involuntary comment: 'And serve him right too.' To which the rest of the meeting concurred!

On one occasion a lady visitor from Liverpool rather rashly invited Phoebe to pay her a visit, never expecting that her remarks would be treated with seriousness, and was not a little embarrassed when she arrived unexpectedly—and on horseback! One can rather imagine the surprise of the lady's genteel neighbours to see this horesewoman dressed, as usual, in a man's woollen coat, a petticoat, several handkerchiefs muffling her head and tied beneath the chin, and a man's hat. It was winter time and for some reason the return journey to Matlock was made on foot.

There is a woodcut of this strange character in one of the early editions of *The Reliquary*, a journal of archaeological and general interest founded and edited by L. Jewitt who lived at nearby Winster Hall. In the portrait Phoebe is shown holding a flute. At her request, a contemporary curate named Gaunt composed an epitaph with 'which she was much pleased.' But it was never inscribed on her gravestone after she died on the 16th May, 1854, or we might have read:

Here lies romantic Phoebe,
Half Gannymede and half Hebe:
A maid of mutable condition,
A Jockey, Cowherd and Musician.

Edward Foster

The Silhouettist

SOME years ago, while on holiday at a seaside resort, I was interested in watching a silhouette artist at work in a temporary studio converted from a corner of a departmental store. He appeared quite oblivious to the attention being paid by a group of bystanders and to the remarks they volunteered from time to time. I was particularly interested in the simplicity of his tools and technique which consisted in cutting the figures out of black card with a small pair of scissors. This he did in triplicate, deftly snipping the outline of eyelashes, nose, lips and chin with remarkable speed, skill and accuracy, and with only brief reference to the shadow cast by his subject. The three shapes were then affixed to mounts and the whole operation completed in a minimum of time, but, of course, with a minimum of detail.

Before the introduction of photography, a silhouette was a popular and reasonably priced 'likeness', sometimes being framed in oval brass mounts to adorn the home, or produced in miniature form for lockets used in personal adornment. The baldness of the silhouette was usually relieved by details suggesting hair style, ornaments, jewellery and dress material, and the artist used a variety of paints and pigments to achieve highlights and other effects.

Derbyshire had a master of this particular art who had a remarkable career and equally remarkable ancestry, and I am indebted to an article contributed to the then *Derbyshire Countryside* by Mr. John Woodiwiss, for much of the following material. Edward Foster was born at Derby on November 8th, 1762. He was descended from Robert Howard, a son of the Duke of Norfolk, and who was among the defeated supporters of James Edward Stuart after the battle of Preston in 1715. Howard succeeded in escaping from the battle and managed to avoid subsequent arrest (a price was placed on his head) by changing his name to Hayward. He eventually settled in Derbyshire where he obtained employment as a gardener and lived a peaceful life. He lived to the age of 104 and his wife to the age of 103 years. A daughter of this union married a Mr. Foster who was employed as a steward of Sir Robert Burdett, of Foremark Hall, and they were parents of Edward who, incidentally, carried on the tradition of longevity by reaching the age of 102 years

Edward appears to have inherited something of his grandfather's martial spirit, for he became an Ensign in the 'Derbyshire Militia at the age of seventeen, later adopting a military career and being gazetted Lieutenant in the 20th Foot (now the Lancashire Fusileers). He served during the concluding stages of the American Revolution under the command of the Marquis Cornwallis and later in the disastrous Dutch campaign under the Duke of York. Foster's regiment then served in Egypt with the task of driving the French out of that country, finally achieving victory at the Battle of Alexandria in 1801. During this campaign Foster suffered a severe eye infection and he was posted home in charge of a draft of sick and wounded soldiers. Upon his recovery he was sent to Walmer, near Deal, where preparations were being made to repulse an expected invasion by Napoleon. Lord Nelson often visited Deal and Foster quite often dined at the same table as the great naval commander.

A few years later he retired from the Army and decided to make a career in art, soon receiving the appointment of 'Miniature Painter to the Royal Family' and occupying rooms in the Round Tower at Windsor. Often he played whist with his royal patrons, expecially Queen Charlotte and the Princess Amelia who used their influence for his advancement. Such a clientele was a sufficient guarantee of success, but within a short time he turned his attention to the work of professional silhouettist, leaving his Windsor quarters and travelling about the country, until he eventually rented a studio at Friar's Gate, Derby, and finally in the Corn Market. His early papier-mache frames had the name Foster superimposed on a crown, and was probably a reminder of his royal appointment. Distinguished clients who were among his sitters included Sir Walter Scott and Lord Byron, besides many other members of the nobility of that time. He also produced a number of the medallion-like portraits worn in broaches and lockets, and a portrait taken when he was 100 years' old shows him wearing one of these ornaments. He invented a mechanical method of reproducing portraits which appears to have been on the lines of a pantograph. His charges ranged from five shillings upwards. Another departure of later years was the publication of educational charts for use in schools. They include 'The Histories of Rome, France and Britain' and 'The Histories of England from B.C. 1100 to A.D. 1852', but these did not achieve a great degree of popularity.

Upon reaching his 100th birthday, Foster was feted by his townsmen who celebrated the occasion with a public dinner presided over by the mayor. In reply to speeches of congratulations and good wishes, the guest of honour spoke of his continued health and testified that he was still in a position to earn his own living. At this time he received a grant of £60 made to him on behalf of Queen Victoria from the Royal Bounty Fund. But the old man, as his centenarian portrait seems to suggest, had known sorrows as well as successes, for he had lost five wives and the sixteen sons they had borne him, and only his daughter, Phyllis, survived. She was born in his 90th year, and followed in her father's footsteps by entering the profession of miniaturist and drawing mistress. She had lived in Huddersfield, Derby and Liverpool where she was resident in 1907, though, like her father in his latter years, in reduced circumstances.

The closing stages of Foster's life were far from happy, for he lived in poverty and debt, and with his faculties failing. He died on March 12th, 1864, and this man—who had enjoyed the friendship and patronage of royalty—was buried in a pauper's grave (No. 28819) in Nottingham Road Cemetery at Derby.

John Smedley

Pioneer of Hydropathy

'I THOUGHT then what a healthy resort it would be for invalids, and had a notion of making it one. My attention during one visit was directed to a little unoccupied villa. It had a capital position, a good supply of water, and a most lovely prospect, but was too small for my purpose. In the meantime a gentleman whose name has become a household word, Mr. John Smedley, was raised up to do great works in Derbyshire. .... It is not my duty here to enquire into the orthodoxy or heterodoxy of Mr. Smedley's views, either as a theraputist or theologian. It is simply the recording of a matter of fact, when I say that the whole neighbourhood was startled, as from a long lethargy, when it saw places of worship rising in every direction at his will and cost; when a hospital for the poor was attached to his factory at Lea Bridge, whilst he went from place to place preaching to crowded audiences under a large portable tent; and when, last of all, he took the little villa at Matlock Bank to which I had given the go-by, but a few years before, and added to it gradually—until now, as you there see it, it is a bulk of buildings large enough for a castle...'

These words were written by a medical man who missed a great opportunity, although a little later, when commenting on the proliferation of centres of hydropathic healing at Matlock, he remarked 'nor is it improbable that, ere this chapter is before the public, I may, myself, have added another to the number, to be conducted, with mild and genial aids, on a plan of my own.' The writer was Dr. S. T. Hall and the book containing the remarks, *Days in Derbyshire*, published in 1863. Whether he ever implemented the plan, I do not know, but he certainly did not make the same impact upon the sick pilgrims who flocked to Matlock as did the man who had no credentials or qualifications in the profession of healing—John Smedley.

Dr. Hall is remembered for his topographical works on Derbyshire, while John Smedley's memorial is the great complex of buildings now devoted to the accommodation of the county offices and the ruined castle—which he personally designed—crowning the summit of nearby Riber Hill. He had planned to build a tower 225 ft. in height as a gift to the nation for an observatory, but it was decided that such a structure in so exposed a position would not be suitable for housing the heavy astronomical instruments required. I recall visiting the castle soon after its abandonment and seeing the interior littered with fragments of broken plaster, fluted marble, carved woodwork, coloured glass and twisted iron tracery—a victory for vandalism over Victorian culture!

John Smedley was born at Wirksworth on June 12th, 1803. His ancestors were engaged in lead-mining, but his grandfather was persuaded to join a relative whose trade was worsted spinning and the manufacture of hosiery. In 1818 the hosiery business was transferred to Lea Mills where John applied himself with diligence and industry to the improvement of the machinery, often being at work before the arrival of his employees and long after their departure. He concerned himself with the health and welfare of his workers, providing them with free medicine, waterproof footwear and clothing, and overnight accommodation in the mill during severe weather conditions. Canteen facilities were provided along with cheap tea, coffee, porridge, and a cook to prepare meat they brought to work. The day's work was initiated by a compulsory religious service (with pay), although there were mild protests when Smedley devised his own prayer-book to lead the devotions.

A biographer wrote concerning the period of Smedley's allegiance to the Established Church:- 'A suggestion that he should re-write parts of the Prayer Book for them was not received with the enthusiasm which he felt it deserved, nor was his criticism, always terse and to the point, much to the taste of the beneficed clergy of the locality. Their view, and his own, of the infallibility of John Smedley were not exactly identical.'

After surviving several periods of acute industrial depression, John prospered sufficiently to achieve more than sufficient wealth for 'ordinary wants' and he and his wife undertook a tour of France, Germany and Switzerland. Upon returning home he was taken ill with typhus fever which he attributed to the great varieties of temperature, unwholesome food and wine, and attacks of malaria. He was so desperately ill and beyond the skill of his physician, that the latter could only commend him to Christ for spiritual blessing; but, although a strict evangelical member of the Established Church, he had a deep conviction of sin for which he could find no formula of forgiveness. His sense of isolation from God was no doubt aggravated by his low physical condition, and he eventually seceded from the Established Church and adopted the principles of nonconformity. There was a marked improvement in his health following an advised visit to Ben Rhydding for hydropathic treatment, and upon his recovery he felt that he had been spared for a purpose. With his usual full-scale commitment to any project he undertook, Smedley travelled around the district with a large marquee in which he conducted evangelical services and urged the principles of total abstinence, having himself signed the pledge in 1853. The result of his revival services found fulfilment in the building of nonconformist chapels at Higham, Holloway, Ashover, Bonsall and Birchinwood near Alfreton. He also provided two schools for Sunday and day education.

His visit to Ben Rhydding in 1849 had resulted in his recovery to health in nine weeks, and caused his complete rejection of orthodox medical practice which at that time did not recognise and accept the theraputic value of hydropathic treatment. Just as he completely renounced his support of the Established Church, although he married Caroline Ann, daughter of the Rev. John Harward, vicar of Wirksworth, so he now whole-heartedly condemned the medical profession. Yet, again, in spite of his avowed antipathy to the profession of medicine, he did not hesitate to recruit Dr. W Bell Hunter as assistant practitioner in his hydro!

Smedley's conversion was so genuine that he dedicated himself, as did his wife, to the free treatment of sick people by hydropathic methods, in addition to seeking to heal their spiritual ills by his preaching ministry. His early beneficiaries were workpeople at the mill and they appeared to have submitted quite meekly to his experimental treatment. After all, it was free! Such was his success with these patients that others in the locality, who had been considered hopeless cases by their doctors, applied for treatment and when some of these were cured the efficiency of the new treatment became noised abroad to a still wider range of sick people. Nor could anyone accuse the Smedleys of seeking financial gain. The enterprise had been started as a philanthropic mission, not as a business speculation, and that was how it was continued for some years.

Perhaps the real pioneer of hydropathy in the district was a Mr. Ralph Davis who lived at Darley Dale, and who had been prescribing this method of treatment. He rented an eleven-roomed house at Matlock for £12 per year, and after it had been in operation for six months John Smedley became voluntary adviser, purchasing the house in 1853 and becoming responsible as its director. This building was soon replaced by a larger one and in 1867 over 2,000 patients were being treated a year, the director and his wife giving of their service with no other reward than the satisfaction that they were following in the steps of One who went about doing good.

Smedley also found time for producing literature other than his *Practical Hydropathy*, writing on such diverse subjects as science, theology and history. He wrote on 'Domestic Fire Apparatus' and 'A Newly Invented Telescope Stand'. Another work was entitled 'The Origin of the English Saxons', while his religious effusions included 'The So-called Reformed Church of England' and 'The Ancient and Modern Church in Britain'. But he devoted most of his time to the improvement of his exclusive system of water treatment, inventing Chile Paste and other health remedies as sidelines to his researches and investigation. His advocacy of nonconformity, non-smoking and total abstinence were incorporated as part of the treatment received, willingly or otherwise, by his patients. Dancing, too, was prohibited. Even the great Charles Haddon Spurgeon was rebuked for smoking on the premises by Smedley. But his interest in the welfare of his patients was such that he maintained personal correspondence with them after their treatment had ended.

The growth of the establishment could not match the demands for accommodation and in 1867 a new building, four storeys high, 200 ft. long and 50 ft. wide was built. Other extensions were carried out in 1881, 1884 and 1886. Charges had to be made for residential patients as the numbers increased, and Smedley wrote: 'The practice here could be made remunerative by much more moderate charges than the terms at Malvern and elsewhere.' In 1872 the 28 years' old Dr. W. Bell Hunter joined the lay practitioner, over-

Opposite:- Top: Left, Edward Foster; Right, William Newton. Bottom: Left, Florrie Carter; Right, John Smedley.

J M BESWICK

J M BESWICK

coming any scruples or prejudices concerning medical etiquette, and two years later he was left to carry on the work as Chief of the Medical Department until his own death at the age of fifty. The Hydro continued to expand after Smedley's death and in 1886 the main front was re-built to match the elaborate and ornate interior. Electric lighting was introduced that year, a generator being installed in the private chapel, while other innovations was a telephone in 1896 and a refrigerator and typewriter the following year. In 1901 a further block was added at a cost of upwards of £11,000.

Among the distinguished pilgrims who came to this shrine of healing were R. L. Stevenson, John Oxenham, T.P.O'Connor, Nat Gould, Ivor Novello, Sir Thomas Beecham, Mark Hambourg, Sir Harry Lauder, George Robey, Jimmy Wilde, General Bramwell Booth, Rev. R.J. Campbell, Rev. C. H. Spurgeon, Sir Arbuthnot Lane, Sir Herbert Baker and Air Marshall Leigh Mallory. Such was the reputation of an establishment founded and developed by a man who had neither medical training nor qualification.

Mrs. Smedley survived her husband for eighteen years. She was a remarkable woman who shared her husband's views without reservation, endorsing his antipathy to medicine and condemning its practitioners as cheats and charlatans. Like her husband she had little respect or tolerance for people whose views happended to be in conflict with theirs, and used rather uncharitable language when expressing opposite convictions. She published a *Ladies Manual* for the respective benefit of married and single women, as well as children of all ages, and confidently claimed to provide 'Certain Relief for every Ailment, Disease, or Injury to which the Human Frame is liable.' She further claimed to be able to cure such major complaints as cancer, tuberculosis, smallpox and rheumatic fever, and strongly condemned the habits of smoking, intemperance and taking snuff, yet it must be admitted that some of her ideas on child-birth, diet and relaxation are in harmony with modern medical teaching and usage, while others might have been conceived by some 17th century alchemist. She contended that thousands of children died as the result of wearing short-sleeved dresses, while the remedy she prescribed for chapped hands was to wear damp gloves night and day. She had a number of remedies for broken hearts, one being to wear a mustard plaster on brown paper the length of the spine while the sufferer had to be kept completely wrapped in blankets. Those contemplating marriage were warned to 'avoid everything, either just before or just after marriage; either walking, riding, eating or drinking, or any exercise which will overheat the body or cause fatigue.'

John Smedley's death occurred on July 27th, 1874, and thousands attended the funeral at Holloway. A 300 ft square memorial window was erected in the Hydro and symbolises Truth seated in a well, holding a mirror and a glass of water, flanked by the figures of Hygea and Asculapius. A memorial hospital was also built to replace the free hospital maintained by Mr. and Mrs. Smedley and a wing was added in 1897 to the memory of Dr. Hunter. Patients paid for their board, but received treatment free of charge. The castle is now a fauna reserve. John Smedley might have composed his own epitaph when he wrote:- 'Life is short with all, and wherever and in whatever way a sphere of usefulness is found which promotes the spiritual and physical welfare of mankind, those who find such a work will find that it brings daily pleasure, with pleasant retrospective and a joyful prospective. It is a work for the benefit of our species, and will last for almost unlimited time when the workers have passed away.'

Samuel Fox

Inventor of the Paragon Umbrella Frame

SAMUEL FOX
The inventor of the Paragon Umbrella Frame
And founder of the extensive Stocksbridge Works
A generous benefactor to the parish of Bradwell
was born in this cottage
June 1815

THIS inscription is mounted on the wall of a cottage opposite Bradwell church. Old photographs show the cottage smothered in a green shawl of ivy which creeps over the stone slates of the roof and wraps itself round the chimney. The cottage formerly incorporated a workshop for the manufacture of weavers' shuttles used in Bradwell's former industries of weaving silk and cotton by the hand loom process. Nearby was a silk mill which occupied Brook Buildings, and, in addition to other weaving factories, many cottages had their pairs of looms during the 18th and 19th centuries. Cotton spinning was also carried on in the locality, including the Bump Mill, near Edentree, a name derived from the fact that 'bump', or course cotton, was manufactured there.

The cottage opposite the church was the home of William Fox whose occupation was that of making shuttles, and it was here in June, 1815, that his son, Samuel was born. Samuel found employment in the wire trade at Hathersage, where, in addition to drawing wire, needles and hackle pins for combing wool and raising the nap on cloth were manufactured. Due to the health hazards, stringent regulations were enforced by the Government to protect the workers from injury during the grinding processes. One company advertised the following mysterious products:- 'cast steel of various qualities, drilled ey'd needles, hand and machine hackles, copper gills of all kinds, combs and porcupines, for flax, wool and silk, comber's broaches, temple teeth, awl blades, fish hooks etc.'

When Samuel reached the age of fifteen, times were hard in Bradwell due to the current depression in lead-mining. An article appeared in the popular London newspaper, *The Sun*, which stated:- 'A numerous and respectable meeting of the inhabitants of the village of Bradwell was held to consider the best means of administering relief to the suffering families in the neighbourhood, especially those who are in indigent circumstances, in consequence of the low rate of wages afforded to those employed in local trades, who, it is well known, cannot by the most difficult exertion earn more than three to four shillings per week. It is impossible to conceive the vast depth of misery which exists. It appeared from the statements of some of the speakers that many of these poor sufferers had their children in bed when visited, whose bedclothes had not a vestige of linen or flannel about them, but was composed of wrappers and old clothes; others had not a little of fire. The respectable inhabitants of the village and neighbourhood subscribed nearly £50, which amount they are actively distributing in coals, meats, and blankets.'

Having served the first part of his apprenticeship at Hathersage, Samuel transferred to Sharrow Moor, Sheffield, to complete the remainder. He was intelligent, hard-working, practical and keen to make progress, soon entering into partnership with a firm at Rivelin Valley. After a while he decided to launch into business on his own account, securing in 1842 a cotton mill, blacking grinding factory and joiner's shop at Stocksbridge. These premises he converted into a wire drawing factory. The speculation proved successful and, with shrewdness and perseverance, and the support of his wife, Samuel gradually increased his output and added to his work force. He experimented with the flexibility of steel wire and applied a hollow type to the manufacture of umbrella frames, which, together with improvements made to the rib terminals, soon usurped in popularity the more cumbersome frames made from cane, whalebone and solid steel. His Paragon Frame Umbrella became a best seller and was soon being exported to other countries.

One writer argued:- 'I should say that Mr. Fox had the Peak to thank for some of his commercial success. He was born in the Peak. There the rain clouds are always gathering. What more natural than that Mr. Fox should turn his attention to umbrellas? He was not one of the umbrella-making chiefs of Tibet, but he was the umbrella-making chief of the world—he was the world's friend, for his paragon frames have and do still shield people of all nations from the wet. They have served other useful purposes too— they have stopped mad bulls, beat dogs, and thrashed erring husbands; and an old Quakeress had such faith in them that, when one of her servants was emigrating, she gave the girl one of Fox's paragon frame umbrellas and a pair of thick boots, saying "Now, Martha, if thou must emigrate thou had better take these. Cling to thy umbrella. It will be a comfort to thee when it's wet, and when its dry thou may want it to drive off some man."'

A less enduring application of his light-weight wire was that used for the frames of crinoline dresses, but this provided a useful source of revenue while the vogue persisted. The name 'crinoline shop' was preserved in the early complex at Stocksbridge. Perhaps this idea of making hoops for crinolines was prompted by his wife who worked in the business with a tirelessness and energy equal to that of her husband. She travelled each Friday to Sheffield to collect the wages and kept a strict control of the accounts. Before he made his own steel, Samuel personally carted the amount required from Deepcar station and then transported the finished products back again. As the business continued to expand, this method became altogether inadequate and he constructed a mile and a half long railway which became the independent Stocksbridge Railway with its own company.

While keeping pace with an international demand for umbrellas, Fox applied himself to providing such industrial requirements as telegraph wires, cable rods and winding ropes for mine shafts. Both he and his wife concerned themselves with the welfare of their workers and many jobs were found for migrants from Bradwell. One particular operation was so dirty that boys engaged in the work were annually supplied with a new suit made by a Sheffield tailor. Upon delivery of the garments, it was customary for the recipients to parade before their benefactor as a gesture of their appreciation of his generosity.

Fox had so keen and perceptive a mind that he was said to be able to weigh up the character and abilities of a candidate for employment by seeing him walk through the yard on his way for an interview. One valued employee, who had proved his worth as a workman, was one day sitting at his bench with his head in his hands. Thinking he was asleep, another workman who concerned himself with other people's business, brought the matter to his master's attention, whereupon he was acidly informed: 'Joseph Hayward is worth more to me asleep than you are when awake.'

Not only did Fox supply employment to many needy Bradwellians, but he anonymously furnished the poorer residents of that village with clothing, food, coals and other provisions during the hard days of winter. And after his death, his liberality was continued by a bequest of £1,000, the interest of which is still disbursed to relieve any cases of hardship or necessity in the village. When the church was built in 1868, Samuel Fox gave £100 towards the project, and also land to enlarge the churchyard and a site for the vicarage. Another Bradwell beneficiary was Horatio Bradwell who left sums of money to several Sheffield hospitals, and also £500 to the National Lifeboat Institution as a donation towards the building of a lifeboat with house, boat fittings, carriage and rocket apparatus, to be named *Ann Fox* and sited between Lynn in Norfolk and Berwick-on-Tweed.

When Fox died on February 26th, 1887, his company employed nearly 2,000 workers, but the enterprise he had pioneered and which became a limited company in 1871, continued to develop and the work population had risen by 1948 to nearly 6,000. And his trade-mark—a fox—is familiar in parts of the world far distant from Stocksbridge—birthplace of the Paragon Frame Umbrella.

Florrie Carter

A Missionary Pioneer

IN the little Wesleyan Reform Chapel on the hillside at Stoney Middleton is a white marble mural recalling the memory of a native of the village who became the first overseas missionary of the Wesleyan Reform Union, an offshoot of the Methodist Church. Her name was Florrie Carter and had she been spared a normal span of years, she might have been as well-known as such heroines of the Faith as Mildred Cable, Mary Slessor and Gladys Aylward. Like Elizabeth Evans, Miss Carter helped—perhaps unwittingly—to pioneer the cause by which women have been given wider recognition in the teaching ministry of the Church.

The story of Florrie Carter is one of heroism, courage and determination, and worthy of being regarded as an epic in Derbyshire history. This brief and rather sketchy biography is somewhat like a pressed flower, lacking in its original colour, fragrance and beauty, but attempting to preserve a shape or shadow of the personality it seeks to memorialise in the frail artistry of words. It is a profile rather than a portrait.

Florrie was born on September 24th, 1875, in a cottage (now demolished) near Stoney Middleton Church. She was the eldest of a family of two daughters and four sons of the village shoemaker and repairer. At the age of four Florrie was sent as a prospective pupil to the Sunday School attached to the parish church, but the officials had a rule which limited membership to children of five years and over and she was sent home. Vexed by this imagined rebuff, the young mother then sent her to the hillside chapel where she was accepted and made welcome. Thus began a family association which still continues and which has been productive of three lay preachers and several Sunday School teachers.

At day school, Florrie proved a bright, intelligent and attentive pupil, and such were her achievements in scholarship that she reached the sixth standard by the time she was eleven years of age. Children in those days were qualified—irrespective of their age—to leave school upon attaining this standard. Moreover, in addition to the fact that opportunities and prospects for advanced education were very limited in rural life, another restricting feature was that of family circumstances, and so the next step in her career was work. Florrie's first venture into the world of employment was that of entering domestic service a short distance from home. She was entrusted with the custody of twin babies, but nursing had so little appeal for the girl that she ran away and found a fresh situation at Riley Farm near Eyam. Here, a good and kind mistress did not prove a strong enough anchorage for her affections and she went to work at Calver Cotton Mill where the hours of employment were from 6 o'clock in the morning to the same hour of evening. One hour was allowed for dinner and Florrie and several workmates devoted part of this time to Bible study.

Here we may perhaps insert a paragraph in parenthesis: a paragraph which illustrates Florrie's affectionate disposition during girlhood. She had been sent on an errand by her father to a tan-yard in Grindleford to fetch a quantity of leather for himself and another shoemaker at Calver. Upon returning home she left her father's parcel and, before continuing to Calver with the rest of the leather, invited her small brother, Tom, to accompany her the rest of the journey. Upon reaching her destination, Florrie was rewarded with the sum of fourpence, and as they were returning home she generously gave her brother a penny. This, however, appeared to be a gross injustice to the little boy, who angrily dashed the despised coin to the ground, refusing to accept anything less than half of the profits. Placing her arm tenderly round Tom's shoulder, she drew him within the comforting warmth of her shawl and patiently said, 'Now, Tom, you can have it all, only let's be friends.' The sequel was that Tom compromised and accepted the half that he had first demanded!

Also at this point we might draw some interesting parallels between Florrie Carter and Mary Slessor, a contemporary who felt the call to missionary service and whose name ranks high in this sphere of Christian work. Both were daughters of shoemakers; both delivered the same tract entitled 'The Monthly Visitor'; both worked in cotton mills from 6.00 a.m. to 6.00 p.m., and both heard the call to West Africa.

As Florrie grew older her interest in Christian work matured and she became a devoted worker at the little Wesleyan Reform Chapel. This interest deepened and developed into a decision made during a mission conducted simultaneously with the Welsh Revival by two students from nearby Cliff College, one of whom was John Harris who was later knighted for his fearless work on the mission field. His name was given nation-wide prominence because of his exposure of atrocities committed under the Belgian administration of the Congo. Missionaries and their sponsoring organisations were bullied into an uneasy silence by the threat that their privileges would be withdrawn if they reported the crimes perpetrated against the native population. Harris refused to be intimidated and relentlessly campaigned for reform, appealing to the British and other humanitarian governments for full investigation of the alleged atrocities suffered by the Congolese. One of the most frequent crimes of which the Belgian authorities were guilty, and which the missionaries were expected to condone, was that of severing the right hands of natives who were unable to pay their quota of gum-copal, rubber or ivory extorted by taxation.

Florrie was greatly influenced by Harris and other students from Cliff College which was then under the direction of the Regions Beyond Missionary organisation, the principal being the Rev. Dr. H. Gratton Guiness. She now had a strong sense of vocation and decided to become a missionary, being accepted as a student at Dorric Lodge, London, a college for women founded by Dr. and Mrs. Guiness. Here she worked so assiduously and with such concentration of purpose, that she completed a three years' course of training in two years. She gained the diploma of the London Obstetrical Society, and carried out her practical training in the east end of London. At the Wesleyan Reform Conference held in 1904 at Foleshill, Coventry, she was ordained as the first woman overseas missionary to be sent out by the Union, setting sail for the Congo on August 26th of the same year.

On June 22nd, 1905, she became wife of the Rev. J. F. Skerritt, another former student of Cliff College, who was working with the Balalo Congo Mission at Ikau. To conform with the regulations imposed by the Belgian authorities, the two missionaries had to make a journey of 1,100 miles down the river before their marriage could be solemnised.

After a pathetically short ministry and married life, Mrs. Skerritt fell victim to fever and died. The same day, because of the torrid climate, her distressed husband was obliged to perform the sad duties of making her coffin, digging the grave, and committing her body to the earth and her soul to the one whom she had served unto the end. Two days after the family at Stoney Middleton had received official notice of their bereavement, the post brought a letter written before she had fallen ill. Much of the content was concerned with an expression of sympathy, affection and anxiety for a colleague on the mission field who had lost her husband as the result of an attack of fever. And on her death-bed, she sent a message to assure those who had contributed to her training and support that their sacrifice had not been in vain.

Sammy Sellors and Thomas Greatorex

A Preacher and an Organist

'AYE', remarked one of a group of quarrymen sharing reminiscences during their morning break, 'Ah well remember him preachin' a temperance sermon i'th chapel at Stoney Middleton when Ah wor a lad. He wor givin' both brewers an' breweries such a thrashin', an' talked abaht many parents squanderin' their money on beer while their little childer, who could neither *walk* nor talk, wor *runnin'* abaht wi' neither shoes nor stockin's on. Then he wound up his sermon by saying that if he could have his way, he'd collect aw th' barrels o' beer, tek 'em to th' top of a hill an' roll 'em dahn into a river at th' bottom. Then he announced his closin' hymn, "Shall we gather at the river?"'

The subject of this conversation was a Peakland preacher named Samuel Wilkinson Sellors who lived in Eyam. Everyone affectionately called him Sammy Sellors. He spoke with feeling and from experience on the evils of strong drink, for, as a young man, he had been pitched out of a swing-boat at the village Wakes while under its influence. On another occasion he had descended a lead-mine shaft to such a depth that the mouth of the shaft looked like a star. Something plummetted past him into the depths; it was a turnip dropped down by an irresponsible mate! Had it struck him he would have been knocked from the climbing ladder and killed. Often he would accompany his father, a local-preacher, to his appointments in neighbouring villages, but while the father was conducting the service at the village chapel, the son was spending the time at the nearest public-house.

But Sammy's sister had predicted, 'If our Sam ever goes to hell, he'll have to tumble over a pile of prayers.' And one day he had his

Damascus Road experience and became one of the most popular preachers in Bakewell Wesleyan Reform Circuit. People who seldom went to chapel were there when Mr. Sellors was planned. One youth, who blew the organ at Cliff College on Sunday mornings, was urged to attend the evening service to hear the celebrated Rev. Samuel Chadwick. 'Not likely,' was the reply, 'Sammy Sellors is preaching at our chapel at Curbar.'

Mr. Sellors had a natural flow of eloquence, although he often pronounced long words phonetically, and lapsed into broad dialect when carried away by his own enthusiasm. He held some unorthodox views and expressed them with an originality which, from other lips, would have seemed gross irreverence. During a discussion on prayer among a group of mourners at a funeral, he expressed the conviction that 'It doesna matter if yo' pray upside dahn the Lord'll sort it aght!'

Some little explanation may be needed to help readers understand the significance of his 'testimony', or experience of conversion, as stated on one occasion during a service. Certain words in dialect are pronounced in the plural as we do in 'crosses' or 'dresses', and the reference was to shoemaker's lasts which, in dialect, become 'lasses'. During his sermon Mr. Sellors recalled how, while at work in his small shoe factory, he felt a sudden constraint to 'kneel dahn among a lot o' rusty owd lasses an' give his heart to the Lord.' Several young women in the choir had great difficulty in restraining their mirth at the implication of Mr. Sellors surrounded by a number of rusty old ladies!

Mr. Sellors disliked debt as much, and as intensely, as he did the Devil. 'If Ah had my way at th' day o' judgment, Ah'd mek them pay up on th' other side as owed money on this,' he used to say. Once he encountered a former resident of Eyam who was paying a return visit.

'Ah've been wanting to see yo' for a long time', he remarked as they shook hands.

'What for Mr. Sellors?' asked the puzzled acquaintance.

'Do yo' remember Ah betted yo' half-a-crown afore yo' left Eyam, an' Ah lost an' never paid yo'?

The visitor confessed that he had no recollection of the incident, but Mr. Sellors insisted upon redeeming the long-standing debt, and the coin was preserved for many years as a souvenir of Sammy Sellors. But he was always strict and business-like in the handling of money, and offered the shrewd advice, 'If an angel gi'es yo' change, allus be sure to count it.'

As a preacher he was quite unpredictable. On one occasion he was preaching at nearby Foolow where the village church and chapel are close neighbours. The church has a solitary bell in its little turret, and this was rung for afternoon service. The chapel service began earlier than that at church, and the monotonous tolling of the bell

Sammy Sellors

Thomas Greatorex

was rather a distraction both to the preacher and worshippers at the chapel where the service was already in progress. Mr. Sellors had struggled valiantly against the competition of the bell as he engaged in prayer. Suddenly he stopped. 'If Ah lived at Foolow Ah'd have that mon stopped', he declared with warmth and then resumed his prayer as if there had been no interruption.

He preached no sugary sermons or honeyed homilies. He was forthright, challenging and sincere. And those who had known him before his conversion could, without hesitation, testify to the sincerity of his religion. One of his own generation, and he was not a non-conformist himself, used to say, 'If ever a man was converted it was Sammy Sellors.'

* * *

Writing in the Derbyshire edition of his *King's England* series, Arthur Mee paid this tribute:- 'It is over a century since Thomas Greatorex played his last organ voluntary, but his name is still with us. Born near North Wingfield in 1758, he came of a family of musicians. His father was a self-taught musician, and his sister was an organist in Leicester when she was only 13. Thomas, very grave and studious, and fond of mathematics and astronomy, soon turned his attention to church music and was organist of Carlisle Cathedral when he was 12.'

The father of Thomas was a nailer by trade, but had such an obsession for music that he taught himself to play the organ. He is said to have built his own instrument when seventy years of age; a claim contested by some writers who contend that his organ was bequeathed by a blind organ-builder. Thomas's sister, Martha, as mentioned by Arthur Mee, was sufficiently qualified to be appointed a church organist at Leicester and had a successful musical career.

Cradled in such an atmosphere of music, it is natural that Thomas should inherit a gift for music as well as an interest in mathematics and science. He was privileged to study in London under Dr. Benjamin Cooke, organist at Westminster Abbey, and became a member of a project entitled the Ancient Concerts when it was established in 1776 and later became its conductor. While still young he became organist at Carlisle Cathedral and also travelled to Italy and Germany, taking singing lessons in Rome and studying music under Pleyel in Strasbourg. But the call of London beckoned again, and he was earning as much as 80 guineas a week in singing tuition fees before he was thirty years' old. He gave as many as 84 lessons a week at one guinea per lesson.

Although his playing was so popular and attracted huge attendances, he did not leave many permanent memorials in the way of personal compositions, for much of his work was never published. He is remembered for his Parochial Psalmody and several hymn tunes which include the still popular 'Tottenham' set to Charles Wesley's 'Being of beings, God of love.' He has been credited with the composition 'Woodlands' set to 'Lift up your hearts, we lift them Lord to Thee', but the Methodist hymn-book compilers attribute this to the later Walter Greatorex (1877-1949). He attended many choral festivals in the capacity of conductor or organist and visited major cities and towns to carry out such engagements.

In spite of his being so absorbed with the occupation of music, his interest in painting, architecture, astronomy, chemistry and mathematics was maintained, and he was awarded the fellowship of the Royal Society in recognition of his invention of a scientific method of measuring the height of mountains. He died in 1831 as the result of a chill caught while relaxing with rod and line, and is buried in the cloisters of Westminster Abbey near his old tutor, Dr. Cooke, and within sound of the mighty organ he had so often provoked to inspire melody.